Phyllis Schlafly Speaks, Volume 2

On Donald Trump

Phyllis Schlafly

Edited by Ed Martin

Permission to quote in critical reviews with citation:
Phyllis Schlafly Speaks, Volume 2: On Donald Trump

ISBN 978-0-9984000-1-3

**Skellig
AMERICA**

TABLE OF CONTENTS

This book is dedicated to John Schlafly, Phyllis' son, who dedicated himself to Phyllis and her work for many decades. If, as some say, there is no President Trump without Phyllis Schlafly, then it can safely be said that John was likewise necessary for the election of Donald J. Trump.

Ed Martin

Editor's Note by Ed Martin

On Friday, March 11, 2016, Phyllis Schlafly welcomed Donald J. Trump to her hometown for a rally at the St. Louis Peabody Opera House. She endorsed Trump for President of the United States saying:

Alright! Hello, everybody! I know who you came to see, and hear, so I'll be quick. I want to welcome the St. Louis crowd. St. Louis is my city. I was born and grew up here, and went to school and college in St. Louis. So, it's a great city, and I welcome you all.

This is the heart of America, and we're happy to welcome a really great American today. I'll tell you about him for minute. I had the chance to meet with him a couple of minutes ago, and I asked him to stand by the Republican Platform, because we have the best conservative platform we've ever had, and he endorses it, he will stand by it, he is a real conservative, and I ask you to support him.

I've worked on the Platform Committee so many times, and I think this is our best one, and we want to maintain it. And it's a great statement for conservatives, and it calls for military superiority. You know, Obama doesn't want us to be superior. He wants to be like everybody else. And I'm confident that Donald Trump will appoint judges like Justice Scalia. That's what we want.

I think he has the courage, and the energy—you know, you have to have energy for that job—in order to bring some changes and to do what the grassroots want him to do. Because this is a grassroots uprising. We've been following the losers for so long. I was on the floor of the (1952) convention when the great Senator Everett Dirksen talked about the kingmakers, and said, "We followed you before and you led us down the road to defeat." But now we've got a guy who's going to lead us to victory! And it's great that he has the endorsement of the best guy in Congress, Senator Jeff Sessions, who knows all about the immigration issue. Donald Trump was the one who has made immigration the big issue that it really is.

Because Obama's trying to change our country. He's trying to fundamentally transform our country, and we don't want him to do it.

This year, we have the candidate who really will give us A Choice Not an Echo! So, please give a big St. Louis welcome to Donald J. Trump.

Phyllis' endorsement of Trump received massive local and national media coverage. It set off a firestorm in Trump opponents' campaigns as they rushed to stop the movement of conservatives to Trump. Four days after Phyllis Schlafly's endorsement, Trump won the Missouri Republican Primary beating favorite Ted Cruz by just 1965 votes out of nearly 1 million cast. Trump went on to win the nomination.

Before Phyllis endorsed Trump in downtown St. Louis, they met privately for what was a joy-filled meeting. Trump thanked her for her support. Phyllis sought his support for the conservative Republican Platform—which he gave. She also asked him to consider only pro-life judges in the mold of Justice Scalia and Trump agreed. Trump closed the meeting by saying he would not let her down.

iii

On September 5, 2016, Phyllis Schlafly died at the age of 92. The next day, her final book, The Conservative Case for Trump, was released and went right onto the New York Times bestseller list. Two months later, Donald J. Trump was elected the 45th President of the United States. On election night at the Trump party in New York City, Senator Jeff Sessions turned to me and said, "Phyllis knew before we did." He then shook his head and smiled, "She just knew."

Phyllis was right. Again.

This volume is the second in a series called Phyllis Schlafly Speaks. Each volume is organized around Phyllis' writings and speaking. Phyllis Schlafly's output as speaker and writer was so vast that it will take us decades to reprint what took her over seven decades in public life to create. We hope you will collect each volume in what will be many volumes. Her wisdom, wit and insight on nearly every subject of historical significance makes it a wonderful challenge for an editor.

Ed Martin

September 10, 2016
She Never Wavered

Delivered by Donald J. Trump at the funeral of Phyllis Schlafly

Thank you very much. What a great honor. And what a great lady. We are here today to honor the life and legacy of a truly great American patriot. I wish first and most importantly to extend my deepest heartfelt condolences to her six wonderful children who she loved so much—John, Bruce, Roger, Liza, Andy, and Anne. And also her sixteen grandchildren and her three great grandchildren.

A movement has lost its hero. And believe me, Phyllis was there for me when it was not at all fashionable. Trust me. You have lost a mother. An amazing mother. And our country has lost a true patriot. Phyllis was a strong, proud, fierce, and tireless warrior; and that's what she was—she was a warrior. And she was a warrior for the country, which she loved so much. Even at the age of 92, this beloved woman had more strength and fire and heart than 50 strong politicians all put together. Believe me, I witnessed it. To borrow a phrase from a great poet, Phyllis was "that strength which in all days moved heaven and earth." This incredible woman has been active in American politics for one quarter of American history—think of that. One quarter of American history. And at the top! She was the ultimate happy warrior—always smiling, but boy could she be tough. We all know that. And in all of her battles, she never strayed from the one guiding principle—she was for America. And it was always America first. People have forgotten that nowadays. With Phyllis it was America first.

She never wavered, never apologized, and never backed down in taking on the kingmakers. She never stopped fighting for the fundamental idea that the America people ought to have their needs come before anything or anyone else. She loved her country, she loved her family, and she loved her God.

Her legacy will live on every time some underdog—outmatched and outgunned—defies the odds and delivers a win for the people. America has always been about the underdog and always about defying the odds. The idea that so-called "little people" or the "little person" that she loved so much could beat the system—often times the rigged system (we've been hearing a lot about it)—that the American grassroots is more powerful than all of the worlds' special interests put together. And that's the way Phyllis felt. She's always felt that way. That's the romance of America; that's the story of the mother and the patriot that we honor here today. Phyllis, who has rejoined with her late husband Fred, is looking down on us right now and I'm sure that she's telling us to keep up the fight—no doubt. No doubt about it.

Phyllis, we love you, we miss you, and we will never ever let you down. God bless you, Phyllis. God bless her family. And God bless everyone. Thank you very much, thank you.

July 14, 2015
Donald Trump Shakes Up the 2016 Campaign

Liberals have perfected the art of exploiting a tragedy for political gain. We've just seen how the massacre of nine people at a Bible study inside a Charleston, S.C. church—apparently committed by a drug-using loser-drifter who dropped out of school after the ninth grade—is being used to bring down the Confederate flag all over the South.

Donald Trump is proving that conservatives can play that game too. Just days after Trump warned that "When Mexico sends its people, they're not sending their best. They're sending people that have lots of problems; they're bringing drugs, they're bringing crime," a young woman was shot and killed while walking with her father after taking pictures at a popular San Francisco tourist attraction.

Francisco Lopez-Sanchez, the Mexican charged with killing Kate Steinle, may not have intended to kill anyone when his stolen gun was fired 3 times. But the larger point is that a Mexican convicted of 7 felonies who had been deported five times should not have been free to walk the streets of San Francisco on July 1.

Rarely has any political candidate been proved so tragically right so soon. But that hasn't stopped furious liberals from trying to make Trump the bad guy, pressuring NBC and other liberal corporations to break Trump's contracts for the Miss USA pageant, clothing at Macy's, and even a celebrity golf outing.

The San Francisco killing was not an isolated event. The very next day in Laredo, Texas, Angelica Martinez was killed with a hammer by Juan Francisco De Luna Vasquez, a Mexican who had been deported four times and twice convicted of entering our country illegally.

Murders are not the only crimes committed by previously deported Mexicans living here illegally. Serious crimes by automobile are also common, as evidenced by several hit-and-run crashes at opposite ends of the country within a week of the killings in San Francisco and Laredo.

In Maricopa, Arizona, on July 4, a woman driving with her two small children was hit and nearly killed by a Mexican illegally driving in the wrong lane. Manuel Perez-Vasquez had been deported to Mexico six times in the past three years; this time Sheriff Paul Babeu plans to hold him as long as possible in the Pinal County jail instead of turning him over to ICE for another "catch and release."

In Raleigh, North Carolina, on July 3, DeShawn and Trazjae Moss were seriously injured when their car was hit head-on by a wrong-way drunk-driving Mexican named Efren Perez-Roblero. Although he was deported two years earlier, had no driver's license and fled the scene of the crash, he was released from jail after ICE determined he did not meet the Obama administration's "current enforcement priorities."

A few days later in Raleigh, Stephanie Johnson was taken to the hospital after she was hit head-on by a truck driven the wrong way by a suspected drunk-driving illegal alien named Antonio Arellano, who had been previously deported after two previous DWI convictions. While Stephanie was lying injured in the street, Arellano ran away from the scene on foot and was arrested two days later, making it impossible to test his blood alcohol.

Although North Carolina is a long way from Mexico, the Tar Heel State seems to attract Mexicans who cause mayhem while driving drunk and then flee the scene. Last November, two students at Wake County Community College were killed and two others injured by Mateo Guzman-Palacios, an unlicensed illegal immigrant from Mexico who had previously been deported three times.

Addressing nearly 10,000 people at the Phoenix Convention Center on Saturday, Donald Trump turned over the microphone to Jamiel Shaw Sr., who told the crowd how his 17-year-old son was cut down by an illegal alien's bullets while walking home in Los Angeles in the early evening of March 2, 2008. Jamiel Jr. was a rising scholar-athlete being recruited by Stanford when Pedro Espinoza shot him. The bullet to the head that killed Jamiel Jr. also penetrated his hand, leading his father to suggest that his son's last words were "hands up, don't shoot."

Most of the Republican establishment, including Mitt Romney and Jeb Bush, have rushed to denounce Trump for raising the issue of criminal aliens from Mexico living in "sanctuary cities," or at least to tone down his rhetoric. Among Republican presidential candidates, only Sen. Ted Cruz and Dr. Ben Carson have welcomed Trump, with Dr. Carson saying, "We need to discuss these things openly. I like people who are willing to say what they believe."

Dr. Carson, who previously fought back against a scurrilous accusation by the notorious Southern Poverty Law Center and forced it to apologize, often says that, "political correctness is destroying our nation." When I evaluate a candidate, the ability to resist liberal pressure is the most important character trait. Trump and Carson are among the few who pass that test.

July 28, 2015
The Sanctuary Scandal

D onald Trump's unorthodox campaign has performed a public service by shining the national spotlight on the problem of "sanctuary cities," which shelter illegal aliens from deportation. The tragedy of Kate Steinle, who died in the arms of her father after being shot by an illegal alien, is that her death was preventable, yet officials have defiantly defended their sanctuary policies.

It wasn't only the City and County of San Francisco that released the seven-times-convicted, five-times-deported Mexican who killed Kate Steinle; Obama's ICE let him go too. ICE has released many thousands of criminal aliens into unsuspecting local communities instead of returning them to their countries of origin, including 121 who were subsequently charged with murdering Americans in the last five years.

According to government figures compiled by Jessica
Vaughan, more than 8,100 deportable aliens (including 3,000
felons) were released by sanctuary cities and counties in just
the first eight months of last year. Some 1,900 of those
wrongly released aliens have already re-offended 4,300 more
times, racking up 7,800 new charges including murder, violent
assault, rape and child rape.

The first local sanctuary policy was officially adopted
more than 30 years ago by Los Angeles' notorious police chief
Daryl Gates. Since then, about 300 cities and counties have
adopted one or more sanctuary policies, such as refusing to
inquire about immigration status when making a traffic stop or
other routine police work; refusing to report a subject's
unlawful status to the appropriate federal agency (now called
ICE); or refusing to honor a "detainer," which is a written
request to detain a subject until ICE can deport him.

Bills to stop local sanctuary policies were introduced in
Congress and state legislatures, but they all wilted under
pressure from amnesty advocates such as businesses dependent
on cheap foreign labor. The U.S. House last week finally
approved a bill to withhold certain federal reimbursements

from sanctuaries, but the promise of a presidential veto assures that even this minor reform will never become law.

Headlines proclaim that Republicans voted to "crack down" on sanctuary cities, but nothing will change unless the restrictions are folded into a must-pass appropriations bill. Washington, D.C., for example, remains a sanctuary even though Congress has the constitutional power "to exercise exclusive legislation in all cases whatsoever" over our nation's capital city.

Local sanctuary policies protect thousands from deportation, but the real damage is done at the federal level. Policies instituted by the administration of Barack Obama have effectively given sanctuary to millions, thanks to Obama's wholesale refusal to enforce immigration laws.

Take Obama's executive amnesty of last November 20, which would have given legal status and work permits (including Social Security numbers) to approximately 5 million of the estimated 11 million illegal aliens. A brave federal judge blocked the work permits, but the 5 million still benefit from

Obama's decision to give them a low enforcement priority, another form of sanctuary.

Obama recently extended lower-priority enforcement to several million more people, and approximately 87 percent of the illegal population—all but 1.4 million of the 11 million—are basically home free, as if the United States is now the sanctuary for the whole world.

Don't assume that illegal immigration has stopped just because the official estimate of illegal population has remained steady at 11 to 12 million for a decade. To replace attrition (a.k.a. self-deportation), illegal immigration (which includes people who enter legally but don't go home when their visas expire) continues unabated at the rate of 1,000 per day.

About 2.5 million people have entered illegally or become illegal since Obama took office on Jan. 20, 2009, and that number doesn't even include legal immigration of over 1.1 million a year. The Census Bureau estimates that "net migration" will bring 14 million new immigrants to the United States during the next ten years.

Of all Obama's sanctuary policies, probably the worst is his vast expansion of refugee and asylum policies. Largely unnoticed by national media, tens of thousands of so-called refugees, mostly from Muslim countries, are being resettled all over the United States.

The United States now receives more refugees than all other countries combined and plops them down in what are called "seed communities" where local opposition is not tolerated. There's even a special federal program to combat "pockets of resistance" such as the recent uproar in Twin Falls, Idaho, where the U.S. government wants to send 300 refugees from war-torn Syria.

The July 16 murders of four U.S. Marines and a U.S. Navy sailor in Chattanooga by a Kuwaiti-born Palestinian are good examples of the dangers of allowing Muslims to enter our country legally as refugees. Like the Boston Marathon bombing by the Tsarnaev brothers in 2013, and like the dozens of Somali young men who have disappeared from Minneapolis, Chattanooga is another case where children of immigrants are radicalized by the terrorist ideologies of the countries their parents came from.

August 18, 2015
Donald Drives the Debate

"I f it weren't for me," Donald Trump told the Fox News moderators at the first Republican presidential debate, "you wouldn't even be talking about illegal immigration." The record-breaking audience of 24 million, which is ten times Fox's usual nightly viewership, had to agree.

Trump's new position paper reinforces the blunt talk that has propelled his rise in the polls: "A nation without borders is not a nation. A nation without laws is not a nation. A nation that does not serve its own citizens is not a nation."

That's a refreshing contrast to the immigration paper recently released by Jeb Bush, who is the candidate of the big-money, big-business faction of the Republican party. Jeb famously said illegal immigrants are guilty only of "an act of love," and his plan would reward them with permanent "legal status," which he said must be "combined with" long-overdue measures to secure the border.

If Jeb's candidacy falters despite the $114 million he raised, the establishment's next choices, Senator Marco Rubio and Ohio Governor John Kasich, have basically similar views. Kasich said the 12 million illegals should be "legalized once we find out who they are," and Rubio said Obama's executive amnesty "can't be terminated because there are already people benefiting from it."

Rubio's statement was made in Spanish on the Spanish-language network Univision, which is reason enough to eliminate him from serious consideration. When somebody is running for president of the United States, why should we have to get somebody to translate his remarks into English?

Trump's new position paper answers his opponents with the plainspoken truth that "America will only be great as long as America remains a nation of laws that lives according to the Constitution. No one is above the law"—including the 300-plus sanctuary cities and counties that openly refuse to help remove illegal aliens even after they commit horrible crimes.

Donald Trump launched his campaign in June by accusing Mexico of sending its worst criminals, murderers, and rapists to live here illegally—a charge that was tragically confirmed by the July 1 murder of Kate Steinle in San Francisco. The rampage continued with the July 24 rape and murder of Marilyn Pharis in her own home in Santa Maria, California; the July 27 attempted rape of a 14-year-old girl and murder of Peggy Kostelnik in Lake County, Ohio, near Cleveland; and the July 29 murders of Jason and Tana Shane of the Crow Nation in Montana—all crimes committed by Mexicans living here illegally who should have been deported for previous crimes.

Having proved his point about crimes by immigrants, Donald Trump's position paper goes on to address the economic harms of unrestricted immigration, both legal and illegal. This subject was introduced to the presidential campaign in April when Wisconsin Governor Scott Walker said immigration should be "based on making our No.1 priority to protect American workers and their wages"—a statement that alarmed Republican donors and the Wall Street Journal's editorial board.

In a section subtitled "Put American Workers First,"
Trump's new position paper elaborates on Walker's idea by
noting that the enormous influx of foreign workers "makes it
difficult for Americans—including immigrants themselves—to
earn a middle class wage." Trump would restrict the admission
of low-earning workers and he would require companies to hire
from the domestic pool of our own unemployed before
importing foreigners to fill "jobs Americans won't do."

As for the millions of people who settled here illegally
since the last amnesty, Trump said without hesitation, "They
have to go. We either have a country, or we don't have a
country."

A recent guest on my weekly radio program, political
expert Steve Deace, emphasized that the "ground game" is
decisive in Iowa, where voters want to shake hands with the
candidates, look them in the eye, and hear them answer
questions about issues that are important to the grassroots.
Iowans seem to like Donald Trump's brash New York style,
and a Nevada poll even has him winning the Hispanic vote
among Republicans.

Trump's high profile assures that the crisis of uncontrolled immigration can't be avoided by presidential candidates of either party. Hillary Clinton's promise to "go even farther" than Obama in granting legal status to millions of illegal aliens has been challenged by Senator Bernie Sanders, who on July 30 denounced the concept of "a completely open border, so that anyone can come into the United States of America. If that were to happen, there is no question that that would substantially lower wages in this country."

September 1, 2015
Anchor Babies on Trial in Texas

A federal case moving to trial in Texas could provide a means to stop the practice of extending automatic U.S. citizenship to children born to illegal aliens. Republican presidential candidate Donald Trump recently called for legislation to end that unpopular practice, which polls show Americans oppose by more than 2 to 1, and even Jeb Bush admitted that it's perfectly legitimate to call those children "anchor babies."

The Pew Research Center estimated that 340,000 children are born annually to citizens of Mexico and other foreign countries who are living illegally in the United States, and that doesn't include children born to "birth tourists," primarily from Asian countries, which the Center for Immigration Studies estimates could be as high as 36,000. These children are called "anchor babies" because their presumed citizenship enables their parents to access a variety of benefit programs intended fur U.S. citizens and makes it so much easier for the entire family to continue living here illegally.

The Texas case is still in its pretrial stage, but an explosive document filed there last week by the government of Mexico adds fuel to the national debate that Trump touched off. The legal brief, which includes a sworn affidavit by Mexico's consul general for Texas, Carlos Gonzalez Gutierrez, openly admits that Mexico's official policy is to encourage its poor people to migrate here illegally in order to access our generous welfare system.

The brief begins by declaring that "Mexico is responsible to protect its nationals wherever they may be residing," and a footnote clarifies that under the Mexican Constitution, "Mexican nationality is granted to children born abroad of a Mexican born parent." In other words, anchor babies born in this country retain their parents' nationality, which means their citizenship belongs there, not here.

Liberals claim that our own Constitution guarantees automatic U.S. citizenship to all children born on American soil, and it's true that the Fourteenth Amendment begins with

17

the words "All persons born or naturalized in the United States
. . . are citizens of the United States." But behind those three
little dots is an important qualification: "AND subject to the
jurisdiction thereof."

What that forgotten phrase means is that when someone
born here is "subject to the jurisdiction" of another nation, that
child does not become a U.S. citizen unless the laws passed by
Congress so provide (and they don't). By filing its legal brief
and submitting sworn testimony in the Texas case, Mexico is
officially declaring that children born to its citizens living
illegally in the United States remain "subject to the
jurisdiction" of Mexico.

The Mexican consul, in his sworn testimony, said that
"My responsibilities in this position include protecting the
rights and promoting the interests of my fellow Mexican
nationals" and "The main responsibility of consulates is to
provide services, assistance, and protection to nationals
abroad." Mexico's assertion of continuing jurisdiction over its
"nationals abroad" is inconsistent with any claim to automatic
U.S. citizenship merely by reason of birth on U.S. soil.

18

The Texas case was filed on behalf of about two dozen mothers who admit they are citizens of Mexico living illegally in Texas. The women complain that without proper ID they cannot get birth certificates for their Texas-born children, and that without birth certificates they can't enroll in Medicaid, food stamps, Section 8 housing, and other U.S. taxpayer-provided benefits.

Like other states, Texas issues a birth certificate to a close relative only upon presentation of a valid ID issued by a U.S. federal or state agency. These restrictions were adopted to combat the growing epidemic of identity theft, whose main cause is the widespread use of forged or fake documents by illegal aliens.

In order to assist its citizens living here illegally who cannot get the required ID, Mexican consulates issue an official-looking document called the matricula consular which includes a laminated photo. Of course, Texas rightly refuses to accept such foreign identity documents which it has no way to verify.

The basic allegation of the lawsuit is that by refusing to accept the matricula consular as proper ID for obtaining a birth certificate, Texas is somehow violating the Fourteenth Amendment by depriving anchor babies of U.S. citizenship. On the contrary, their reliance on a foreign identity document proves they are "subject to the jurisdiction" of a foreign power and thus not eligible for automatic U.S. citizenship.

The Texas lawsuit was concocted by a group called the South Texas Civil Rights Project, which was founded in 1972 as a spin-off of the ACLU. It was assisted by another leftwing legal outfit, Texas RioGrande Legal Aid, whose largest supporter, the Legal Services Corporation, collected $375 million of U.S. taxpayer funds in the current fiscal year.

September 23, 2015
2016 Candidates and Education

Education has become a critical issue for 2016 presidential candidates. Even Donald Trump, in his speech at Trump Tower announcing his candidacy, made a point of declaring that "Common Core is a disaster. Education has to be local." But Jeb Bush, whose foundation took millions from Bill Gates and Pearson to promote Common Core, remains unmoved by grassroots opposition. Two years ago, Jeb insulted parents concerned about Common Core as people who are "comfortable with mediocrity." Jeb actually praised the heavy-handed federal role in public education by saying, "I think Secretary Duncan and President Obama deserve credit for putting pressure on states, providing carrots and sticks. I think that's appropriate." Bush doesn't realize that Secretary Duncan's and President Obama's practice of trying to strong-arm states into accepting ridiculous Common Core standards is totally inappropriate.

In the 2016 election, Americans must hold the candidates accountable for their views on education. Candidates should be asked where they stand on the Every Child Achieves Act and the Student Success Act, which try to replace No Child Left Behind with more legislation that removes local control from schools. Candidates should be asked if they support schools controlled by parents *or* if they favor schools that are bound by Common Core's obnoxious standardized tests.

Education should not be pushed to the back burner in the 2016 election. Eagle Forum knows that the quality of education our students receive fundamentally determines the future of America. Because of this, we have created a "STOP Common Core Pledge" so voters will know who will stand up against bad policies in education. We need a president and Congress who will oppose any attempt to reauthorize a federal role in public education.

September 28, 2015
Real Cases of Illegal Immigrant Crimes

O nly a few days after Donald Trump warned of the dangers that illegal immigrants pose to the American people, a young woman named Kate Steinle was shot and killed by an illegal immigrant while walking with her father after taking pictures at a popular San Francisco tourist attraction. The San Francisco killing was not an isolated event. The very next day in Laredo, Texas, Angelica Martinez was killed with a hammer by Juan Francisco De Luna Vasquez, a Mexican who had been deported four times and twice convicted of entering our country illegally.

Murders are not the only crimes committed by previously-deported Mexicans living here illegally. Serious crimes with automobiles are also common, such as hit-and-run crashes at opposite ends of our country within a week of the killings in San Francisco and Laredo. In Maricopa, Arizona, on

July 4, a woman and her two small children were hit and nearly killed by a Mexican illegally driving in the wrong lane. Manuel Perez-Vasquez had been deported to Mexico six times in the past three years; this time Sheriff Paul Babeu plans to hold him as long as possible in the Pinal County jail instead of turning him over to ICE for another "catch and release."

In Raleigh, North Carolina, on July 3, DeShawn and Trazjae Moss were seriously injured when their car was hit head-on by a wrong-way drunk-driving Mexican named Efren Perez-Roblero. He had been deported two years earlier, had no driver's license, and fled the scene of the crash. However, he was released from jail after ICE determined he did not meet the Obama administration's "current enforcement priorities." Last November, two students at Wake County Community College were killed and two others injured by Mateo Guzman-Palacios, an unlicensed illegal immigrant from Mexico who had previously been deported three times. It's time that Americans acknowledge these facts instead of ignoring them.

October 6, 2015
The Establishment Looks for a New Plan B

T he Republican Establishment designed the process to deliver the 2016 presidential nomination to a business-friendly moderate who avoids so-called social issues. The consultants who rewrote the party rules after 2012 are now trying to explain to their patrons what went wrong and how to fix it.

Plan A, of course, was to assure the nomination of Jeb Bush, whose views are the perfect reflection of the Republican donor class. But despite many months of campaigning, $114 million of political funds raised through June 30, and two presidential debates watched by a record-setting average of 24 million people, Jeb Bush has dropped to sixth place, registering only 4 percent in the latest Pew poll.

One reason for Jeb's poor performance is that he never learned from Ronald Reagan's example how to prepare for a presidential campaign after his narrow defeat at the 1976 Convention in Kansas City. Reagan traveled the country speaking to small audiences of grassrooters and fielding their questions.

The immigration issue, and the way it has grabbed the attention of the grassroots, made it difficult for Jeb Bush to secure the Republican Party nomination in the usual way. Bush will continue to try, of course, and may be able to play insider politics to line up more endorsements and donors with wads of political money.

But the kingmakers always have a Plan B if their first choice stumbles. In 1964, for example, Pennsylvania Governor William Scranton was carefully groomed as a second-choice alternative who could jump in the race after Nelson Rockefeller failed to stop the conservative Barry Goldwater.

Speculation has been in the media that Marco Rubio, Scott Walker, or Chris Christie is the Plan B for the Establishment in case Jeb Bush fails to gain popular support. But Rubio is tied for only fifth in Iowa and fourth in New Hampshire, Christie has failed to gain any real support and Walker has dropped out completely.

The abrupt withdrawal of Scott Walker is the clearest indication of the Establishment trying to regain its control of the process. Walker admitted that his early withdrawal is part of a donor-driven strategy to "clear the field in this race" to pave the way for an "alternative to the current frontrunner" (Donald Trump)—and, he said, "I encourage other Republican presidential candidates to consider doing the same."

Walker insisted that candidates should have a "positive" message and that only "candidates who can offer a positive conservative alternative to the current frontrunner" should be considered. He stressed that "Ronald Reagan was good for America because he was an optimist," and complained that "the debate taking place in the Republican Party today is not focused on that optimistic view of America."

Contrary to Governor Walker, who may not have realized that the words "positive" and "optimistic" are consultant code for "business as usual," every poll shows that the voters, by a margin of nearly 3 to 1, say the country is on the "wrong track" or headed in the "wrong direction." Those voters don't need more happy talk; they're looking for a candidate who's willing and able to turn the country around and "make America great again."

When Jeb Bush and some of these other candidates tried criticizing Trump, polls showed that any loss in support for Trump simply went to another outside-the-Establishment candidate, such as Ben Carson or Carly Fiorina. So Plan B is striking out as badly as Plan A did.

It may be that the only alternative left for these Republican would-be kingmakers is the late entry of a new candidate to enter the race. We are already hearing rumblings about resurrecting Mitt Romney.

On the Democratic side, Vice President Joe Biden has been considering whether to enter the race, so it is obviously not too late for a new candidate to emerge. Indeed, an entirely new candidate could be nominated as late as the Republican National Convention next summer in Cleveland, as occurred at the famous Republican convention of 1880.

The grassroots must be vigilant to anticipate and counter the attempts by Republican insiders to impose an unwanted candidate on the American people. When we fought for and nominated Barry Goldwater in 1964, we did not win the general election that year but we built the conservative movement and laid the foundation to win five out of the next six presidential elections.

When the Establishment is allowed to pick the Republican nominee, a candidate unable to win the support of the all-important middle-class America results. Establishment candidates have been unable to win the popular vote in five out of the last six elections, and that outcome is not something any Republican should want to repeat.

October 7, 2015
Trump Makes Immigration a Big Issue

D onald Trump's position paper on immigration addresses many of the immigration problems that Americans are concerned about, including the economic harm of unrestricted immigration, both illegal and legal. This subject was introduced to the presidential campaign in April when Wisconsin Governor Scott Walker said immigration should be "based on making our No.1 priority to protect American workers and their wages." This statement proved to be very alarming to Republican donors and the Wall Street Journal's editorial board. In a section subtitled "Put American Workers First," Trump's new position paper elaborates on Walker's idea by noting that the enormous influx of foreign workers "makes it difficult for Americans— including immigrants themselves—to earn a middle class wage." Trump would restrict the admission of low-earning workers and he would require companies to hire from the domestic pool of our own unemployed before importing foreigners to fill jobs that Americans supposedly will not do.

As for the millions of people who settled here illegally since the last amnesty, Trump said without hesitation, "They have to go. We either have a country, or we don't have a country." The American people are rewarding Trump for his conservative position with his rise in the polls; a Nevada poll even has him winning the Hispanic vote among Republicans.

Trump's high profile assures that the crisis of uncontrolled immigration cannot be avoided by presidential candidates of both parties. Hillary Clinton's promise to "go even farther" than Obama in granting legal status to millions of illegal aliens has even been challenged by the socialist Senator Bernie Sanders. It's a good thing that Donald Trump is discussing important issues that might not otherwise be discussed in the 2016 campaign.

October 8, 2015
Trump Promises Immigration Crackdown

Donald Trump's immigration position paper reinforces the blunt talk that has propelled his rise in the polls. He attracted many voters with statements like: "A nation without borders is not a nation. A nation without laws is not a nation. A nation that does not serve its own citizens is not a nation." That is a refreshing contrast to the immigration paper released by Jeb Bush, who is the candidate of the big-money, big-business faction of the Republican party. Jeb famously said illegal immigrants are guilty only of "an act of love." Jeb Bush's plan would reward illegal immigrants with permanent "legal status."

Donald Trump's new position paper answers his opponents with the plainspoken truth that "America will only be great as long as America remains a nation of laws according to the Constitution. No one is above the law." His paper details how he would put this principle into practice by taking action against the 300 sanctuary cities and counties that openly refuse to help remove illegal aliens even after they commit horrible crimes.

Donald Trump launched his campaign in June by accusing Mexico of sending its worst criminals, murderers, and rapists to live here illegally—a charge that was tragically confirmed by the July 1 murder of Kate Steinle in San Francisco. The rampage continued with the July 24 rape and murder of Marilyn Pharis in her own home in Santa Maria, California and the July 29 murders of Jason and Tana Shane in Montana. All of these crimes were committed by Mexicans living here illegally who should have been deported for previous crimes. Hopefully, Trump's bold stance on immigration will prompt other candidates to come out in favor of immigration policies that benefits American citizens.

November 24, 2015
Governors Say "Not in My State!"

Defying the wishes of the American people, President Obama remains determined to import tens of thousands of poorly screened Muslims as refugees from the civil war in Syria and scatter them in communities across America. Taxpayer-funded agencies are ready to help the refugees gain access to welfare programs and enroll their children in local public schools.

After FBI Director James Comey told Congress on Oct. 22 that his agency is unable to vet Syrians adequately, the House of Representatives voted by over two-thirds (289 to 137) to add an extra layer of screening to the refugee resettlement process.

Almost two-thirds of the nation's governors (31 out of 50) have told the president not to send Syrian refugees to their states without assurances that the influx would not become a

Trojan Horse. Even New Jersey Governor Chris Christie, who helped re-elect Obama in 2012 with a well-timed gesture of support during Hurricane Sandy, told the president that "I will not accept any refugees from Syria."

Obama's response to this groundswell of public opinion was to lash out with peevish petulance. Speaking in Turkey, which is 98 percent Muslim, Obama said, "When I hear folks say that maybe we should just admit the Christians but not the Muslims, that's shameful. That's not American. That's not who we are." A few days later in Malaysia, where Islam is the official state religion, Obama said that a preference for Christian refugees would constitute "prejudice and discrimination" that "helps ISIL and undermines our national security."

Since Christians are the most widely persecuted group in the Middle East, you'd expect that Christians would be more likely to qualify as refugees, which requires demonstrating a "well-founded fear of being persecuted." Yet of the 2,184 Syrian refugees Obama has already allowed to come here during the past four years, only 53 (or 2 percent) are Christian and 2,098 (96 percent) are Muslim, according to State Department statistics.

After Donald Trump called for a "database" of Muslim immigrants, Dr. Ben Carson said "we should have a database on everybody who comes into this country. I want to know where they came from, I want to know where they're going and why they're here."

Databases do exist but, as Trump says, our government lacks "good management procedures" to insure that visitors to our country follow the law. It's estimated that half of the 11-plus million illegal aliens failed to leave when their time was up, even though they are on a government database.

It's ludicrous to think that our government can effectively screen refugees from Syria or from any Muslim country. Consider the following security breaches that were reported in just one week since the Paris attacks on Friday, Nov. 13:

On Saturday, Nov. 14, three Syrian men were stopped in the Caribbean island of St. Martin after arriving on a flight from Haiti. Using fake Greek passports, they had already flown from Europe to Brazil, then to the Dominican Republic, then Haiti.

On Monday, Nov. 16, eight Syrians in two family units (two men, two women, and four children) were caught illegally entering the United States from Mexico as they crossed the Juarez Lincoln Bridge in Laredo, Texas.

On Monday, Nov. 16, six young men (five from Pakistan and one from Afghanistan) crossed illegally from Mexico into Arizona near Tucson. They were captured 16 miles inside our border, and Sheriff Paul Babeu warns that "terrorists are— using well-established smuggling routes to come across the border."

On Tuesday, Nov. 17, five young men from Syria were detained in Honduras after arriving from Costa Rica on their way to Guatemala and onward through Mexico to the United States. They were using stolen Greek passports which had been doctored to replace the original photos with photos of the Syrians.

On Wednesday, Nov. 18, a Syrian woman was stopped in Honduras and sent back to El Salvador after flying on a Greek passport. On Thursday, Nov. 19, another Syrian woman was arrested in Costa Rica after flying there from Peru with a fake Greek passport.

On Thursday, Nov. 19, eight tough-looking young men from Morocco were arrested at the airport in Istanbul claiming to be tourists, but carrying maps and directions to Germany. Turkish authorities believe the men were being smuggled by ISIS to join the fight in Europe on behalf of the Muslim caliphate.

On Friday, Nov. 20, five Syrians, consisting of one family unit and two additional males, crossed the international bridge from Mexico into the United States at Laredo, Texas.

On Saturday, Nov. 21, a Syrian woman and two Pakistani young men without passports were detained by officials in Honduras after they entered that country by bus from Nicaragua, presumably bound for the United States.

As a fitting conclusion to a week of broken borders, on Friday, Nov. 20, the Obama administration petitioned the Supreme Court to overrule the lower federal judges who blocked his executive amnesty of five million illegal aliens.

Tell your elected public officials to just say no to Syrian refugees.

December 15, 2015
Donald Trump Channels Pat McCarran

Donald Trump's presidential campaign has done it again. Speaking aboard the USS Yorktown on the 74th anniversary of the Japanese attack on Pearl Harbor, Trump called on our government to stop letting Muslims enter the United States "until our country's representatives can figure out what the hell is going on."

Trump's profanity was justified by the revelation that the Muslim wife who helped her Muslim husband massacre 14 people in San Bernardino received a visa from our government, which gave her official permission to enter the United States last year. With that visa and her Pakistani passport, she legally traveled from Saudi Arabia to San Bernardino and married her U.S.-born Pakistani fiancé, with whom she jointly plotted jihad against Americans.

Before Tafsheen Malik received that valuable visa from our government, she was supposed to be screened for terrorist sympathies. A week after the massacre, FBI Director James Comey told Congress he still didn't know if she was given the required personal interview or what questions she was asked.

Now that it's too late to keep her out, we're learning that Tafsheen left a long trail of jihadist rants on social media which were overlooked by the U.S. consular officials who granted her visa. We learn from the New York Times that "anti-American sentiment in Pakistan was particularly high" following the raid that killed Osama bin Laden and that "it is often difficult to distinguish Islamist sentiments and those driven by political hostility toward the United States"—in other words, anti-American attitudes were not enough to keep a Pakistani Muslim out of the United States.

Other presidential candidates rushed to disavow Trump's proposal, which they claimed was illegal, unconstitutional, or "not who we are," echoing a sanctimonious phrase that President Obama has used 46 times.

Unconstitutional? On the contrary, the Supreme Court
has never dared to limit Congress' "plenary power" over
immigration, even when it was based on race, religion or
national origin. In a 1977 case, for example, the Supreme Court
observed that "the power to expel or exclude aliens [is] a
fundamental sovereign attribute exercised by the government's
political departments largely immune from judicial control."

That plenary power is best expressed in this federal
law: "Whenever the president finds that the entry of any aliens,
or of any class of aliens, into the United States would be
detrimental to the interests of the United States, he may by
proclamation, and for such period as he shall deem necessary,
suspend the entry of all aliens or any class of aliens as
immigrants or nonimmigrants."

That law was the work of one of our greatest U.S.
senators, Pat McCarran (D-NV), after whom the airport in Las
Vegas is named. Along with Representative Francis Walter (D-
PA), the two Democrats wrote the McCarran-Walter
Immigration Act which Congress passed over Harry Truman's
veto in 1952.

All throughout the Cold War, McCarran-Walter was successfully used to keep out aliens who were members or "fellow travelers" of the Communist party or members of "Communist front" organizations. In 1980, the same law was used by President Jimmy Carter during the Iran hostage crisis to suspend visas to anyone who wanted to come here from Iran.

In addition to barring the entry of "any class of aliens" who may be "detrimental to the interests of the United States" (a category that could include Muslims or persons of any faith who are citizens of, or have traveled to, a Muslim country), the law says the president may "impose on the entry of aliens any restrictions he may deem to be appropriate." They could be required to wear ankle bracelets to monitor their movements, or to provide passwords to their electronic devices and social media accounts, as a condition of the privilege of entering our country.

Sixty years ago, the Democratic party could boast a patriotic, pro-American anti-Communist like Pat McCarran, but that is no longer the case. Hard-left Senator Pat Leahy (D-VT) proposed an amendment, which unfortunately was adopted by the Senate Judiciary Committee with the help of seven

Republicans, stating that "It is the sense of the Senate that the United States must not bar individuals from entering into the United States based on their religion, as such action would be contrary to the fundamental principles on which this Nation was founded."

No, the fundamental principle on which this nation was founded is that "we the people," through our elected representatives, have the unalienable right to pick and choose whom we shall allow to enter our great country. The Constitution which our founding fathers bequeathed "to ourselves and our posterity" does not extend its rights and benefits to the whole world.

January 19, 2016
Will the Republican Establishment Stand Down?

As Republicans prepare to cast their first presidential ballots in Iowa and New Hampshire, the field remains dominated by "outsider" candidates Donald Trump and Ted Cruz, while Establishment favorites Jeb Bush, Chris Christie, John Kasich and Marco Rubio have been unable to advance to the finals. Will the Republican kingmakers and consultants who picked every nominee since Reagan (Bush, Dole, Bush, McCain and Romney) step aside to let the grassroots, also known as the "base," work its will this year?

After months of waiting for Trump to self-destruct, the Washington-based Republican Establishment has finally found a way to take back control of the party from the outsiders and grassroots. The plan revolves around the newly empowered House Speaker, Paul Ryan, who is openly contemptuous of Trump and has little use for Cruz.

To signal his intentions, Ryan tapped South Carolina Governor Nikki Haley to give the official Republican response to President Obama's final State of the Union address. Haley admitted she cleared her remarks with the Speaker, who then let it be known that she would be a fine choice for vice president.

With Ryan's blessing, Haley used her national platform to slam the "angriest voices" in the presidential campaign and disavow the Republican front-runner's popular call for a temporary pause in Muslim immigration. She seemed to be responding more to Trump than Obama, so it's no wonder that her speech was praised by Obama's press secretary and the White House chief of staff.

The Spanish-language version of Haley's response was delivered by Congressman Diaz-Balart, who was also selected by Speaker Ryan. According to a translation provided by the Miami Herald, Diaz-Balart promised that Republicans would work toward "a legislative solution … to those who live in the shadows" (i.e., amnesty), and would also "modernize the visa system and push the economy forward" (i.e., import even more low-wage guest workers).

46

Ryan then led Republicans on a two-day retreat with an "aspirational agenda" of "inclusiveness and optimism," which is meant to be a direct contrast to the campaign themes of Trump and Cruz. Much favorable press coverage describes Ryan as a "counterweight to Trump" or the "anti-Trump" who wants to give the eventual nominee a "platform to run on."

Memo to the Speaker: the official Republican platform will be written and adopted by delegates to the national convention, most of whom are disappointed with the ineffectiveness of the Boehner-Cantor-McCarthy-Ryan Congress. As a veteran of past platform writing committees, I promise that this year's delegates will have no use for Ryan's open-borders ideology, which holds that anyone who can find a low-wage job should be allowed to settle in the United States.

Paul Ryan obviously resents the rise of Trump and Cruz and would do anything in his power to prevent either from winning the nomination, but could he influence the convention? To answer that question, consider a remarkable article in the Wall Street Journal by the kingmakers' top lawyer, Ben Ginsberg.

47

Ginsberg predicts "pure chaos" if the convention opens on July 18 with no candidate holding a majority of the delegates, and he suggests plausible scenarios by which the Establishment kingmakers could try to manage a "chaotic" convention to produce a nominee acceptable to them. The RNC needs to "be sure that the arena and hotel rooms are available if the convention goes more than four days," which hasn't happened in my lifetime.

To see what can happen at a deadlocked convention, consider the Republican convention of 1880, which ran for seven days because none of the three leading candidates could reach a majority. After 34 failed ballots the convention finally turned to a "dark horse," nominating Congressman James Garfield for president and Chester Arthur for vice president, neither of whom was even running when the convention opened.

Ben Ginsberg understands the critical importance of convention rules and credentials for boxing out the grassroots in favor of the Establishment candidate. That's what happened at the 1952 Republican convention, where I watched the kingmakers steal the nomination for Dwight Eisenhower by unseating delegates pledged to the Republican favorite, Senator Robert A. Taft.

Ginsberg admits he wants to change the infamous Rule 40 which he wrote in 2012 to prevent a second candidate (Ron Paul) from being placed in nomination at Mitt Romney's convention. If no candidate wins on the first ballot, delegates are no longer bound to vote for their state's primary winner and are free to support a "dark horse" who never competed in a presidential primary or participated in a televised debate.

That's how "dark horse" Paul Ryan could become our nominee. Such an outcome could destroy the Republican Party and guarantee a Democratic victory by causing disheartened grassroots voters to stay home and tempting an aggrieved candidate to mount a third-party or independent presidential campaign.

January 25, 2016
Keeping Track of Refugees

After Donald Trump called for a "database" of Muslim immigrants, Dr. Ben Carson said, "we should have a database on everybody who comes into this country. I want to know where they came from, I want to know where they're going and why they're here."

Databases do exist but, as Trump says, our government lacks "good management procedures" to insure that visitors to our country follow the law. It's estimated that half of the 11-plus million illegal aliens failed to leave when their time was up, even though they are on a government database.

It's ludicrous to think that our government could effectively screen refugees from Syria or from any Muslim country. Consider some of the following security breaches that were reported in just one week after the Paris attacks last November:

On Nov. 14, three Syrian men were stopped on the Caribbean island of St. Martin after arriving on a flight from Haiti. Using fake Greek passports, they had already flown from Europe to Brazil, then to the Dominican Republic, then Haiti. Three days later, five more young men were detained in Honduras, also using stolen Greek passports. They were on their way to the United States through Mexico.

On Nov. 16, six young men (five from Pakistan and one from Afghanistan) crossed illegally from Mexico into Arizona near Tucson. Sheriff Paul Babeu warned that "terrorists are using well-established smuggling routes to come across the border." On Nov. 19, eight tough-looking young men from Morocco were arrested at the airport in Istanbul claiming to be tourists, but carrying maps and directions to Germany. Turkish authorities believe the men were being smuggled by ISIS to join the fight in Europe on behalf of the Muslim caliphate. Tell your elected public officials to just say no to Syrian refugees.

February 1, 2016
Donald Trump's Constitutional Moratorium

W hen Donald Trump was standing on the USS Yorktown on the 74th anniversary of the Japanese attack on Pearl Harbor, he called on our government to stop letting Muslims enter the United States "until our country's representatives can figure out what the hell is going on." Trump's profanity was justified by the revelation that the Muslim wife who helped her Muslim husband massacre 14 people in San Bernardino received a visa from our government, which gave her official permission to enter the United States in 2014. With that visa and her Pakistani passport, she legally traveled from Saudi Arabia to San Bernardino and married her U.S.-born Pakistani fiancé, with whom she jointly plotted jihad against Americans.

Before she received that valuable visa from our government, she was supposed to be screened for terrorist sympathies. A week after the massacre, FBI Director James

Comey told Congress he still didn't know if she was given the required personal interview or what questions she was asked.

Tafsheen left a long trail of jihadist rants on social media which were overlooked by the U.S. officials who granted her visa. We learn from the New York Times that "anti-American sentiment in Pakistan was particularly high" following the raid that killed Osama bin Laden and that "it is often difficult to distinguish Islamist sentiments and those driven by political hostility toward the United States."

The Supreme Court has never limited Congress' "plenary power" over immigration, even when based on race, religion or national origin. In a 1977 case, for example, the Supreme Court ruled that "the power to expel or exclude aliens [is] a fundamental sovereign attribute exercised by the government's political departments largely immune from judicial control."

February 2, 2016
America's "Last Chance"

O n the eve of the Iowa caucuses, where the first ballots for the next president are cast, Senator Jeff Sessions (R-AL), who has not endorsed a candidate, gave a round of interviews declaring that 2016 "is the last chance for the American people to take back control of their government."

"This election is different because we have pell mell erosion of law, the constitutional order, where President Obama has pushed an agenda that eviscerates the immigration legal system, and pushed this trade agreement that will commence decades of transferring American economic power to an ever-expanding international commission. It's just not going to stop."

"This is the way the European Union began," he added. Daily news reports are now vividly describing how the EU is disintegrating, making Americans mighty glad we never joined any proposed North American Union.

Europe has been in an uproar for months over Germany's decision to admit 1.1 million refugees, mostly young men of fighting age from war-torn countries, and German Chancellor Angela Merkel has finally started to backtrack from that reckless decision. Merkel announced that refugees will be sent back home after the war is over in their homeland, and she even suggested that border guards should shoot at migrants who try to enter Germany illegally.

In Britain, meanwhile, Prime Minister David Cameron has been trying to get permission from the EUrocrats to impose a four-year waiting period for the most generous welfare benefits, in order to discourage new immigrants from other EU countries. A spokesman for the grassroots organization called Leave EU points out that even if Cameron's proposal were approved, "we are not even asking for an end to the supremacy of EU law over national law, genuine control over migration or independent representation on global bodies and the power to make our own trade deals."

Our nation's sovereignty depends on control of both immigration and trade, and that's why Senator Sessions urges voters to choose a candidate who promises to kill the Trans-Pacific Partnership trade deal with nearly a dozen Asian nations. A new study by economists at Tufts University predicts that U.S. ratification of the TPP would shrink our GDP by $100 billion, leading to a loss of 448,000 American jobs.

"This election will be the last chance for Americans to get control of their government," said Sessions, after 30 years of promises to end illegal immigration. "I think this election is the big one."

"To win, Republicans need to demonstrate that they care about the average person who goes to work every day," he added. Average Americans are tired of paying billions in welfare handouts to immigrants who are undermining U.S. wages.

"People should have total confidence and a clear commitment on those issues. If they don't, then they don't have my vote," he said.

The importance of Sessions' statements on key issues in the presidential race, especially immigration and TPP, should not be underestimated. Sessions warned that, if the next president approves the TPP, it would put our trade with Asia under a powerful international commission on which the United States would have just one vote.

Our immigration policy has been anti-American, decade after decade, and the voters need to know that 2016 might be our last chance to elect a president who can reduce this tide of illegals crossing our borders. The interests of working Americans, their jobs, their wages, their hospitals, their schools, and the public safety, must "be put first," Sessions urged.

"We need a president with the credibility to tell the world that the time of illegality is over. Do not come to this country unlawfully," he said.

"Make sure—because this could be the last chance— that the vote you cast is for a person who is going to, with courage and steadfastness, fix the immigration system that's so broken and is impacting adversely Americans' safety, their wages, their hospitals, their schools, those kind of things," Sessions said during an appearance on the Howie Carr radio program, which is heard throughout New Hampshire.

"And also we need to know with absolute clarity: are you for or against the Trans-Pacific Partnership," he added. "It must not pass."

"This may be the last opportunity the American people will have to have their will imposed and create a lawful immigration system that serves the national interest," Sessions emphasized. "I know we have to talk about the economy, national security, and the military, and the budget, and it's hard to know who's got the best idea," Sessions said.

"But on these two issues [immigration and TPP], I think the voters should say, 'If you're not going to be right on those, I'm not voting for you in this primary and I'm not going to vote for you as president.' I really think it's that important."

February 23, 2016
How Common Core Ended the Bush Dynasty

As Republicans try to make sense of Donald Trump's huge victory in the South Carolina primary, the big news is the shellacking of Jeb Bush in a state that voted four times for a George Bush for president. Trump defeated Jeb by the overwhelming margin of 4-to-1 (33 percent to 8 percent).

When Jeb suspended his presidential campaign following his humiliating rebuke by South Carolina's Republican voters, it was more than just a personal disappointment. It marked the end of the Bush family's 25-year campaign to remake public education according to federal standards.

Exactly one year ago, before he announced running for president, Trump was asked on Hugh Hewitt's radio talk show:

"What does Donald Trump think about Common Core?" He replied, "Well, first of all, I think it's going to kill Bush."

Hewitt expressed surprise, so Trump explained: "For people in Washington to be setting curriculum and to be setting standards for people living in Iowa and other places is ridiculous. People don't want to have somebody from Washington looking down and saying this is what you're going to be studying."

That interview was four months before Trump launched his presidential campaign with his sensational promise to make Mexico pay for a wall on our Southern border. Although his warnings about Mexican and Muslim immigration drew the most attention, Trump continued to denounce Common Core in all his campaign speeches and one of his few campaign ads was devoted to it.

One year later, it's clear that Trump was right: not only that it's "ridiculous" for "people in Washington" to be setting curriculum and standards for "what you're going to be studying"—but he was equally right to foresee that Common

Core would "kill" any chance of returning the Bush family to the White House.

It all began in 1988 when then-Vice President George H.W. Bush, hoping to succeed Ronald Reagan, declared that he wanted to be "the education president." Bush adopted that label in order to define himself as what he would later call a "kinder, gentler" conservative than Reagan.

After his election to what many viewed as "Reagan's third term," Bush summoned the 50 state governors to attend a two-day education summit in Charlottesville, Virginia. The 1989 Charlottesville summit, underwritten by major corporations such IBM, launched the basic idea that later became Common Core: national standards for what is taught, enforced by measures of "accountability" to ensure that all schools toe the official line.

That summit made a little-known Arkansas governor named Bill Clinton into a national figure big enough to run for president, and when Clinton ousted Bush 41 from the White House, he pursued the same education policies he helped develop at Bush's Charlottesville summit. Helped by wife

Hillary's board membership on a corporate-funded outfit called the National Center on Education and the Economy, Clinton rebranded Bush's America 2000 as Goals 2000.

Then George W. Bush emerged with his own campaign as a "compassionate conservative" using the slogan "leave no child behind." Bush's No Child Left Behind law picked up right where his father and Bill Clinton left off—with the same standards-and-assessment model of federal control.

When the failures of No Child Left Behind became too obvious to ignore, the same failed ideas were repackaged by the National Governors Association under the label Common Core. Although the NGA is a private, corporate-funded lobbying organization with no power over public schools, the Common Core was quickly adopted by 46 states and the publishing industry rolled out new textbooks supposedly "aligned" to the Common Core.

The Common Core was promoted heavily by Jeb Bush's Foundation for Excellence in Education, which received large gifts from charities controlled by Bill Gates,

Michael Bloomberg, Rupert Murdoch, and Pearson PLC, the world's largest textbook publisher.

As Common Core became toxic, Jeb made a too-little, too-late attempt to rebrand the same ideas under a new name. Last month he issued a new education position paper described as "a blueprint for a 21st century American education system" which he said was "the great civil rights challenge of our time."

Putting education reform under the mantle of "civil rights" was the tip-off that federal control would continue in any Jeb Bush administration. Once something is declared to be a matter of "civil rights," states aren't allowed to experiment or deviate from uniform rules enforced by the federal government.

The runner-up candidates in South Carolina, Senators Ted Cruz and Marco Rubio, have also spoken out against Common Core, although both senators were absent on December 9 when the Senate voted to extend federal control over local schools for another five years. Hopefully, the Republican Party has returned to its pre-Bush position against any federal role in public or private education.

March 7, 2016
500,000 Visa Overstays in 2015

I llegal immigration is too important for the American people to ignore. Donald Trump made it one of the major issues of his presidential campaign. Many conservative favorites have promised to build a wall along the southern border, increase border patrols, and make other important changes. Those are all great ideas. However, sneaking across the border is not the only way that illegal immigrants get into this country.

A report from the Department of Homeland Security revealed that more than 500,000 immigrants on temporary visas overstayed their time in our country. That figure does not even include overstays on student visas or workers visas. Thousands of these illegal immigrants came from countries with known terrorist ties such as Iran, Iraq, Yemen, Pakistan and Libya. In a meeting of the Senate Subcommittee on Immigration and the National Interest, Chairman Jeff Sessions explained: "Visa expiration dates have become optional. The Obama administration does not believe that violating the terms of your visa should result in deportation. What we are witnessing is tantamount to an open border. Millions are free to come on temporary visas and no one is requiring them to leave."

Senator Sessions is right to sound the alarm about these disturbing reports. Terrorist attacks on American soil are becoming a great threat. All President Obama wants to do is take away guns from law-abiding citizens. This will not solve the problem. The best way to stop terrorist attacks is to enforce our immigration laws to prevent terrorists from getting here in the first place. I applaud Senator Sessions for holding the Department of Homeland Security accountable. Even one terrorist in the United States has the potential to threaten many American lives. Thousands of illegal immigrants from terrorist countries pose a threat that cannot be ignored.

It's the duty of the Department of Homeland Security to enforce visa expiration dates to protect American lives.

March 15, 2016
Candidates Turn Against Trade Deals

T he first question asked of the presidential candidates at the most recent Republican debate, hosted by CNN in Miami on March 10, was "whether trade deals have been good for the American workers." Moderator Jake Tapper observed that one of Donald Trump's "signature issues" has been his criticism of "disastrous trade deals" that have destroyed many good middle-class jobs that existed a generation ago.

The other three GOP candidates have supported trade deals in the past and still support them in principle, even while acknowledging the voters' concerns about the harmful effects of such agreements. Two of the candidates even advocate the 12-nation Trans-Pacific Partnership (TPP), which President Obama wants Congress to ratify before he leaves office.

Ohio Governor John Kasich likes to remind everyone that he "grew up in a blue collar family," but votes he cast during his 18 years in Congress helped to decimate the manufacturing base of his home state. Kasich voted for NAFTA in 1994, and in 2000 he voted to grant the "normal" trading privileges which allowed China to enter the World Trade Organization.

Florida Senator Marco Rubio twice voted in favor of giving President Obama the authority to negotiate trade agreements including the Trans-Pacific Partnership (TPP). He insisted that trade deals provide "access to foreign markets" (even though most of the world's people can't afford to buy anything made in America) and he offered sentimental happy-talk that American workers "can compete against anyone in the world" despite 20 years of trade deficits proving otherwise.

Senator Ted Cruz once voted in favor of presidential trade authority before reversing himself on the subsequent vote last year. Cruz now says he opposes the TPP, but Congress has never rejected a trade deal after giving the President the authority to negotiate it.

"I am different in one primary respect, and that's trade," Trump insisted in the debate, explaining that "trade deals are absolutely killing our country." He has proposed tariffs to offset abusive practices such as currency devaluation by "certain countries that are taking advantage of the United States and laughing at our stupidity."

In response to Trump's suggestion that we threaten to tax imports from countries that do not trade fairly with us, Ted Cruz warned that Americans would be forced to pay higher prices for Chinese-made goods at Walmart. "Honestly, it's just the opposite," Trump retorted, because "we will start building those factories and those plants," and "people will buy products from here, rather than buying it through China where we're being ripped off."

A new study by the non-partisan National Bureau of Economic Research provides support for Trump's criticism of free trade with China. This new report, entitled "The China Shock," shows how trade with China has resulted in higher unemployment and lower wages in communities across our country.

Last year imports from China rose to a new record high of $481.9 billion, while the Chinese purchased less than a quarter of that amount from the United States. The nearly $500 billion we sent to China last year could have supported millions of good jobs for Americans, but instead some of it ends up financing the Chinese military to point its missiles at California.

According to the 200-year-old theory of free trade, workers who lose manufacturing jobs to China should be able to find new jobs in other industries that benefit from a trade surplus, such as the pharmaceutical industry, or in non-tradable industries such as medicine and legal services. But millions of these workers, many of whom are men struggling to support their families, have not found adequate replacement jobs.

Some settle for lower-paying jobs, while others give up entirely, creating a social issue as well as an economic one. The percentage of men between 25 and 54 years old who are not employed has tripled in the last half century, and many who had been working at $40 per hour manufacturing jobs are now receiving only $10 per hour jobs at Walmart or fast-food joints.

Michigan, where the original "Reagan Democrats" were identified as a voter group, shattered its 40-year record for turnout in a presidential primary this year, and some precincts even ran out of ballots. Trump walked away with a double-digit victory over his nearest Republican rival, while Hillary Clinton was humiliated by an upset defeat by Senator Bernie Sanders, a critic of free trade.

In the general election in November, there will be millions of voters ready to cast their ballots for a candidate who stands up for American workers rather than catering to lobbyists who seek free-trade deals. CNN documented 45 times that Hillary pushed for the disastrous Trans-Pacific Partnership, which the leading Republican candidate opposes.

May 10, 2016
No Third-Party Candidate

E very four years there is political chatter about trying
to run a third-party candidate who will supposedly
be more conservative than the Republican nominee.
The lesson is the same every time this is tried: third-party
candidates do not win because the United States is a two-party
country.

The grumblings we hear about Donald Trump are
mostly because of his strong stand against illegal immigration.
Party bosses know that if Trump wins and then shuts down
illegal immigration and so-called free trade, it will cost the
Democratic Party millions of future votes and cost Republican
businessmen lucrative deals for themselves with foreign
countries.

Despite how current immigration heavily favors
Democrats, many church leaders who usually lean Republican

dislike Trump's strong stance against illegal immigration. They oppose Trump's plan to build a wall and deport illegal aliens.

They assume that more immigration puts more people in their pews, and most churches have a mission to bring the faith to people of all nations. Trump's nationalistic tone, to make America great again, is not something likely to be heard from a church pulpit.

Yet rank-and-file churchgoers overwhelmingly support Trump's views against current levels of immigration and trade. Evangelical voters, in particular, preferred Trump over his rivals in the Republican primaries, and they will surely vote heavily in favor of Trump rather than Hillary in the general election.

Despite the opposition of their members, some church leaders persist in supporting permissive immigration and opposing Trump. In sharp contrast with their congregations, they are more likely to agree with Obama on immigration than with Donald Trump.

Two years ago, officials from several conservative
Christian denominations met with President Obama in the Oval
Office and gushed their support of his "immigration reform."
Obama's phony "reform" means legislation that would grant
citizenship to illegal aliens and do little to stem the flood of
illegal immigrants into our nation.

The immigration issue may be preventing some church
leaders from siding with Donald Trump now. While opposition
to Trump is expressed in moral terms—even though they had
no trouble supporting the divorced Ronald Reagan in 1980—a
real motivation is that church leaders do not want Trump's
criticism of immigration.

The prior Republican nominee for president, Mitt
Romney, stridently criticized Donald Trump earlier this year
and still refuses to endorse him. This should not be a surprise
because Romney had harshly criticized Trump's statements
about immigration during the campaign.

Rev. Luis Cortes, as president of an Hispanic Christian
network and nonprofit legal organization that helps
immigrants, declared after the White House meeting that "the

entire religious community" supports an Obama-style immigration reform package. "For the first time ... all the major denominations and churches and religious bodies of this country believe that it is a moral imperative that we get immigration reform done," he asserted.

But churchgoing voters indicated otherwise during the Republican primaries by nominating Donald Trump. Now is the time for church leaders to listen to their own flock on the important issue of immigration.

The amount of immigration allowed by a nation is a political matter, not a religious one, and this issue has become the elephant in the room—impossible to overlook. The stunning election results in Austria two weeks ago demonstrate that those who try to duck or downplay the immigration issue are headed for defeat.

As in the United States, the leaders of both major political parties in Austria ignored the problems caused by immigration. A candidate emerged there named Norbert Hofer, who campaigned on "putting Austria first" despite the media giving him little chance of winning.

On April 24th, Austrians voted with a large turnout and the candidate opposed to permissive immigration won the first round in a stunning double-digit landslide. The two major parties that had echoed failed immigration policies, as Democrats and Republicans here have done, fared so poorly that they failed even to qualify for the upcoming runoff, which the Trump-like Austrian candidate is also expected to win.

Church leaders should recognize that responsibility is just as important as charity. No church would urge people to unlock their doors at night in order to allow anyone in, and we should not persist with open borders to welcome hordes of illegal aliens who include many hardened criminals.

When an unwelcome "neighbor" comes into our home, we "deport" him out of our house, and Trump's leadership on the immigration issue has earned him the support of millions of Democrats and Republicans alike. Loving our neighbor does not mean unlocking our doors to any and all comers.

There will not be a third-party candidate who is as good as Trump on immigration. There will be only two viable candidates to choose from this fall, only one of whom will safeguard our country against immigration, and Jesus will not be on the ballot.

June 7, 2016
Put the Wall in the Platform

T he promise to build a wall along America's southern border with Mexico has carried Donald Trump to his remarkable victory in the Republican primaries for president. Now it's time to put that promise into the official Republican Party Platform.

Many would be surprised to learn that a border security fence or wall was not already in the Republican platform. After all, President George W. Bush signed the Secure Fence Act which Congress passed in 2006 with the support of many Democrats including then-Senators Barack Obama and Hillary Clinton.

In the 10 years since Bush signed that law in a staged photo-op, the government has actually built only 36 miles of secure double fencing instead of the 700 miles authorized by that bipartisan, high-profile law. As a result, our southern border is penetrated daily by wave after wave of drug smugglers, human traffickers, people with incurable or infectious diseases such as the Zika virus, and even Muslims and Chinese people who somehow made their way to Mexico.

Business lobbyists and the U.S. Chamber of Commerce, who hold too much influence in the Republican Party, oppose a wall because it would interfere with their continued exploitation of cheap foreign labor at the expense of American workers. In addition to tolerating the flow of illegal labor, the Chamber wants to expand every category of visas for foreign workers, both skilled and unskilled.

According to Politico, Republican power brokers have convened "as many as 10 closed-door huddles with business lobbyists to discuss the party's platform." Attendees were warned not to discuss details with the press, but you can bet that building a wall was not on their agenda.

The big-business lobbyists also expressed alarm at Trump's promise to "discourage companies from moving jobs outside the United States." One participant said his colleagues are "pretty much aghast" at Trump's proposals to protect

Americans against rampant cheating by our so-called "trading partners."

House Speaker Paul Ryan, meanwhile, has been developing his own agenda for Republicans in an effort to compete with Trump's. Under the slogan "A Better Way," Ryan's proposals include old chestnuts like cutting taxes, entitlements and regulations, but nothing about limiting immigration or the hemorrhage of jobs to foreign countries.

The Ryan agenda is basically the same as what Jeb Bush and 15 other failed presidential candidates campaigned on, but those ideas obviously didn't sell to the Republican electorate. The voters have spoken, and the future of the Republican Party starts with a wall along our southern border.

Even some members of the Republican National Committee are resisting the wall as a political statement that belongs in the party platform. One RNC member called the wall "a symbolic thing" rather than "a physical thing," while another member said the border wall is not to be taken "literally" because "it is a metaphor."

The two RNC members are right that the border wall would be a powerful symbol, but only if and when it is actually built. Once completed, the wall on our southern border would stand as a "metaphor" for the fact that coming to America requires the invitation and permission of the American citizens who are already here.

The 2012 platform has many good provisions, including opposition to "any form of amnesty" and support for states using their authority to enforce federal immigration laws. But building a wall is now the foundation of Republican immigration policy—and yes, Mexico will pay for the wall.

Yet the Chamber of Commerce calls it a "myth" that "building a wall along the U.S.-Mexico border, and deporting all undocumented immigrants from the United States, would enhance national security." The Chamber's analysis asserts that a border security wall would cost between $15 and $25 billion to build, and not even $1 billion to maintain, but those are small sums compared to the real costs of illegal immigration.

The federal, state, and local costs of criminal justice to process and incarcerate criminal aliens is at least $15 billion a year, not to mention the harm caused by those crimes, such as horrific crashes that have occurred when smugglers drive the wrong way on freeways at night with their headlights turned off. Even deportation is not as expensive as opponents of border security pretend.

A wall along the border would reduce illegal immigration and cause real wages to increase for average American workers for the first time in more than a decade. That may not be something the U.S. Chamber of Commerce wants for big business, but it's something that would attract American workers to vote Republican.

⤬

June 28, 2016
Brexit Stuns the Globalists

Britain's decision to "leave" the European Union (EU) ended the career of Prime Minister David Cameron, who had campaigned hard to "remain" in that supranational body of unelected bureaucrats. Small-c conservatives in Cameron's own Conservative Party rebelled against the liberals and globalists who dominate both major parties over there. Sound familiar?

Everyone agrees that Donald Trump is the big winner of the vote. As the New York Times conceded, the "leave" voters are "eerily similar to Donald Trump's followers, motivated by many of the same frustrations and angers."

Trump, who just happened to land in Britain as the results were announced, was quick to draw the obvious parallels. He promised that, "Americans will have a chance to vote for trade, immigration and foreign policies that put our citizens first. They will have the chance to reject today's rule by the global elite."

Imagine if the Republican Party were stuck with yet

PHYLLIS SCHLAFLY SPEAKS, VOLUME 2

citizens first.

citizens first. They will have the chance to reject today's rule by the global elite."

Imagine if the Republican Party were stuck with yet another Bush as its presumptive nominee instead of Donald J. Trump. From the first George Bush's foolish declaration of a "new world order" on September 11, 1990 to the second George Bush's obsessive attempts to promote economic integration within the Western Hemisphere, the Bush family is committed to a globalist ideology which the English-speaking people on both sides of the Atlantic have firmly rejected.

Soon after he became president, George W. Bush traveled to Quebec City in April 2001 where he called for "hemispheric integration"—in other words an economic union, like the European Union, for 34 countries of the Western Hemisphere. Bush committed his administration to negotiating a Free Trade Area of the Americas (FTAA) that would become effective no later than 2005.

When his grand vision of hemispheric integration was foiled by the rise of anti-American rulers in Venezuela and Bolivia, Bush repackaged his globalism in the form of a North

American union, which he launched in Waco, Texas in March 2005. That meeting of the "three amigos" had the goal of expanding NAFTA from merely a "free trade" agreement to a closer political union among the three countries of North America (the United States, Canada and Mexico).

The specter of a North American Union, modeled on the European Union, was aggressively pushed by one of the three amigos, Mexican President Vicente Fox, who recently was back in the news for using a vulgar epithet against Donald Trump. Wall Street Journal editor Robert Bartley wrote of Fox: "There is one voice north of the Rio Grande that supports his vision. To wit, this newspaper."

The Bush-Fox vision of a unified North America was given glossy support by numerous think tanks including the Council on Foreign Relations (CFR) whose 70-page report, "Building a North American Community," called for "the extension of full labor mobility to Mexico." The CFR report was co-authored by Senator Ted Cruz's wife Heidi, who wrote: "I support the Task Force report and its recommendations."

Given Bush's support for "full labor mobility" between the United States and the corrupt, violent, drug-trafficking nation across our southern border, it's no wonder that Bush was also an advocate of "comprehensive immigration reform," i.e., giving amnesty to millions of illegal Mexican immigrants, which our Congress wisely rejected in 2006, 2007 and 2013. Among the British people who voted to leave the European Union, the biggest reason was the EU's complete failure to control the flood of immigrants from Asia, Africa and the Middle East.

The powerful "breaking point" poster was widely distributed by the campaign to "leave" the EU. The poster showed an actual photograph of Europe's insecure border at its weakest point in Slovenia, showing a column of thousands of illegal immigrants, extending far off in the distance as far as the eye can see, with the caption: "The EU has failed us all. We must break free of the EU and take back control of our borders."

Senator Jeff Sessions (R-AL) recalled that the 1979 election of Margaret Thatcher as Prime Minister of Great Britain was an early sign of the 1980 wave that swept Ronald

Reagan into the White House. "Now it's our time," Sessions said, to defeat "the establishment forces, the global powers" that "want to erode borders, rapidly open America's markets to foreign produced goods, while having little interest in advancing America's ability to sell abroad."

July 5, 2016
Trump's Muslim Ban Gains Support

When an ISIS-supporting Muslim named Omar Mateen massacred 49 people at a nightclub in Orlando on June 12, Donald Trump reminded Americans that he is still the only political candidate to support a pause in the massive flow of Muslims entering the United States. Trump made his proposal last December after another ISIS-supporting Muslim massacred 14 people at an office Christmas party in San Bernardino, California.

Trump said his Muslim ban would be temporary. "Until we are able to determine and understand this problem and the dangerous threat it poses," he said, "our country cannot be the victims of horrendous attacks by people that believe only in Jihad."

Trump's reasonable, commonsense proposal was immediately condemned or disavowed by other presidential candidates in both parties. Even Senator Ted Cruz said he disagreed with it, though he didn't say why.

Now that Cruz has returned to his "day job" as U.S. Senator from Texas, he recently co-authored a new report with Senator Jeff Sessions that provides powerful support for Trump's position. The report issued June 22 shows that the overwhelming majority of convicted terrorists came into our country as immigrants or refugees from Muslim countries.

Cruz and Sessions were able to determine the birthplace of 451 of the 580 individuals who were convicted of terrorism since the 9/11 attacks on September 11, 2001. Some 380 of the 451, or 84 percent of these terrorists, were foreign born—and most of them came from Muslim-majority countries such Pakistan, Egypt, Lebanon, Yemen, Somalia, Iraq and Afghanistan.

Of the 71 terrorists who were born here, most were children of immigrants or refugees from Muslim countries, although the senators could not report the exact number because the Obama administration refused to provide that information. Despite four official letters from the U.S. senators on August 12, December 3, January 11 and June 14 to the appropriate agencies of the U.S. government, Obama's appointees have refused to answer questions about the immigration status of the 580 persons convicted of terrorism in the United States since 9/11.

Coming six months after San Bernardino, the Orlando massacre entitled Donald Trump to say "I told you so" and he did so in a powerful speech on June 13. "We admit more than 100,000 lifetime migrants from the Middle East each year," Trump said. "Since 9/11, hundreds of migrants and their children have been implicated in terrorism in the United States."

Trump was right to include the children of immigrants as part of the immigration problem. The Orlando shooter Omar Mateen was born in the United States, but a witness said he referred to Afghanistan as "my country."

Besides Orlando, other mass killings have been perpetrated by the U.S.-born children of Muslim immigrants or individuals who were brought here as children by their Muslim parents. Examples include one of the San Bernardino killers;

the Fort Hood shooter, Major Nidal Hasan; the Tsarnaev brothers, who bombed the Boston Marathon in 2013; and the man who killed four active-duty Marines and a sailor in Chattanooga in 2015.

Don't overlook the Muslims who entered the United States on the pretext of marriage, such as the Pakistani woman named Malik who helped her husband commit the San Bernardino massacre. The Orlando shooter's first wife, his second wife, and his second wife's first husband were all Muslims who never should have been allowed to come here.

In an interview, Trump said, "there's no real assimilation" by Muslim immigrants, even in the "second and third generation." A liberal website called Politifact tried to refute that statement by citing a telephone survey of Muslims who said they wanted to become American, but the interviews were conducted in "Arabic, Farsi and Urdu"—hardly evidence of assimilation.

Other countries have recently experienced terrorist massacres directed or inspired by the Islamic State, including 130 murdered in Paris; 32 in Brussels; 45 at the airport in

Istanbul, Turkey; 28 at a restaurant in Dhaka, Bangladesh; and, most recently, 200 in Baghdad, Iraq. Obviously we can't prevent atrocities in other countries, but we can and should prevent potential terrorists from coming here.

Obama, however, is doing just the opposite. He has admitted over 5,000 so-called refugees from Syria this fiscal year and scattered them to 167 communities in 39 states. More than 99 percent of the Syrian refugees are Sunni Muslims, and only eight individuals identified themselves as Christian. The Obama "surge" of Syrian refugees is on track to reach 10,000 by September, even though FBI Director James Comey told Congress last year that there's no way to vet them adequately.

Most Syrians lack the skills to support themselves without government assistance, and Robert Rector of the Heritage Foundation calculates that 10,000 refugees will cost federal, state and local taxpayers some $6.5 billion over their lifetime. If that's not bad enough, Hillary Clinton has vowed to increase the number of Syrian refugees to 65,000.

July 12, 2016
Trump Battles Globalist Republicans

Before heading to Cleveland to accept the Republican nomination for president, Donald Trump paid a high-profile visit to Capitol Hill, where he hoped to unify Congressional Republicans behind his presidential campaign. Many of the 247 Republican representatives and 54 senators were cordial to their party's presumptive nominee, but others remained hostile and weren't shy about expressing it to reporters after leaving the closed-door meetings.

One Congressman reportedly demanded that Trump promise to protect Congress' Article I powers if he is elected. Trump tactfully refrained from pointing out how many times the Republican Congress has unilaterally surrendered its Article I powers, including the power "to regulate commerce with foreign nations."

Senator Jeff Flake of Arizona openly mocked Trump at the meeting and then bragged to reporters about their "tense" exchange. Flake, an unrepentant member of the Gang of Eight that produced the 2013 amnesty bill, has already announced plans to resurrect that discredited bill next year no matter who is elected president.

Trump's next stop was a private meeting with Senator Ted Cruz, who inappropriately brought his campaign manager Jeff Roe to the meeting. Two months after suspending his campaign, why does Cruz still utilize a high-priced campaign manager to join high-level discussions with the presumptive nominee?

The answer is that Cruz never stopped running for president, and the people who spent $158 million—more than twice what Trump spent—to back Cruz in 2016 are not going away. Cruz recently set up two new nonprofit organizations to keep his key people employed, prematurely launching another run for president in 2020.

Cruz's delays in endorsing Trump and his disloyal preparations to run for president in 2020 help only one person:

Hillary Clinton, which is what some Republican mega-donors actually prefer because they are globalists who oppose Trump's stances against immigration and free trade.

The globalists will never accept Trump or anyone else who puts Americans first, and they are using Cruz to undermine Trump's campaign. Cruz's mega-donors think they can buy their way to control of the Republican Party even if Trump wins the presidency this year, and they are already funding the takeover of several conservative organizations.

These globalist moneymen are also hostile to our Constitution, which they want to rewrite in a new constitutional convention, also called "Convention of States." Eric O'Keefe, who has close ties to the billionaire Koch bothers, backs the Never Trump movement and is a board member of the Convention of States project.

Justice Scalia in May 2015 called this attempt for a new constitutional convention a "horrible idea," but several of its cheerleaders were able to get on the Republican platform committee that is meeting this week. Cruz has praised the delusional proposal to add many amendments to the

94

Constitution, and some of his donors are part of the same group that seeks to alter our Constitution.

Cruz earned support by many conservatives when he first came to D.C. four years ago. It is long overdue for Cruz to repudiate the support of these globalists who are working against Trump and against our national sovereignty.

"We will no longer surrender this country or its people to the false song of globalism," Trump promised in his April 27 foreign policy speech in Washington. That sentiment is anathema to the globalists who provide much of the money for Republican candidates.

"I am skeptical of international unions that tie us up and bring America down," Trump continued. "Under my administration, we will never enter America into any agreement that reduces our ability to control our own affairs. Americans must know that we're putting the American people first again."

When Trump vows to "put Americans first," the globalists complain about "protectionism," as if there's something wrong with expecting our own government to protect American jobs and America's economic interests.

"On trade, on immigration, on foreign policy, the jobs, incomes and security of the American worker will always be my first priority," Trump said. "Both our friends and our enemies put their countries above ours, and we—while being fair to them—must start doing the same."

In a June 22 speech in New York, Trump intensified his attack on the globalist money interests: "We'll never be able to fix a rigged system by counting on the same people who have rigged it in the first place. The insiders wrote the rules of the game to keep themselves in power and in the money."

"It's not just the political system that's rigged, it's the whole economy," Trump continued. "It's rigged by big donors who want to keep wages down. It's rigged by big businesses who want to leave our country, fire our workers, and sell their products back into the United States with absolutely no consequences for them."

We've waited a long time for a Republican candidate to express these pro-American views, but Donald Trump's victory in the presidential primaries proves they are what the voters want to hear.

July 19, 2016

How Pence Complements Trump

When Donald Trump introduced Indiana Governor Mike Pence as the vice presidential nominee, the media had a field day unearthing Pence's past tweets and votes that appeared to disagree with his future running mate's positions. On issues such as free trade agreements, some of Pence's past views seemed closer to those of his former colleague, House Speaker Paul Ryan, than his new running mate.

But on one of Trump's signature issues—his opposition to the resettlement of Muslim refugees from Syria—the Indiana governor took Trump-style executive action even before Trump. Way back on November 16, Governor Pence directed his state agencies to suspend payments to the agencies that profit by redistributing tax money to people from Syria.

Pence took that prompt and decisive action after it was revealed that at least one of the Muslim terrorists who massacred 130 people in Paris, France on November 13 had slipped into that country by posing as a Syrian refugee. Pence also relied on the October 21 testimony of FBI Director James Comey before the House Committee on Homeland Security.

Comey told Congress that it's simply not possible to vet Syrian refugees adequately because there are no reliable documents or databases for those people. "We can query our database until the cows come home, but there will be nothing show up because we have no record of them."

For Pence's swift action to protect American citizens against the demands of foreigners, he was sued by one of the agencies that spends our tax money to resettle refugees. On February 29, an Obama-appointed federal judge named Tanya Walton Pratt blocked Pence's order on the absurd basis that he was discriminating against Syrian refugees on the basis of their national origin.

Governor Pence appealed the Obama judge's decision on April 11. Contrary to the claim that our government spends two years vetting Muslim refugees for terrorist sympathies before letting them in, Pence's brief quoted an April 7 story by the Associated Press reporting, "While the resettlement process usually takes 18 to 24 months, the surge operation will reduce the time to three months."

Pence has tweeted his opposition to a complete Muslim ban, but he may change his mind by checking the polls. A series of recent polls proves that most Americans strongly or somewhat support temporarily banning all Muslims from entering our country.

In just the last month, a Reuters/Ipsos poll, an NBC News-SurveyMonkey poll, a Morning Consult poll, and a Fox News poll all found that Americans support Donald Trump's proposal even if they don't support him. These polls show that substantial numbers of Democrats, African-Americans, and people who voted for Obama in 2012 support a temporary ban on Muslims or people from Muslim-majority countries.

Those polls were completed before the most recent terrorist horror in Nice, France, which resulted in the mass murder of 84 and the injury of 200 more when Mohamed

Bouhlel intentionally ran over them with his truck. The terrorist's apparent targeting of women, children, and families, as he drove his truck in zigzag fashion to kill them, has horrified millions.

The threat of terrorism is not the only reason to stop the refugees, who are bringing tuberculosis (TB) in both its active and latent varieties. TB is one of six "comeback" diseases that had been virtually wiped out in our country but are returning with refugees; the others are measles, mumps, whooping cough, scarlet fever, and bubonic plague.

The same judge ruled against another of Pence's most important initiatives. On June 30, she issued a preliminary injunction against an Indiana law signed by Governor Pence that bans abortion solely for the reason of the child's sex, race or disability (including but not limited to Down syndrome).

In India and China, abortion of baby girls based on their gender results in a disproportionate number of births of baby boys. This provides an additional reason to oppose immigration from these countries, because we do not want any immigrant groups that have far more men than women.

The same judge who blocked Pence's proper actions concerning refugees and abortion also ruled in 2011 that Indiana could not stop tax money going to Planned Parenthood. How does it happen that a single Obama-appointed judge can block the enforcement of a state legislature and governor?

Trump recently experienced firsthand the overreaching by federal judges when Supreme Court Justice Ruth Bader Ginsburg lashed out against Trump in comments that she has since expressed regret for saying. Apologies aside, Justice Ginsburg's comments illustrated how politicized the federal judiciary has become, and both Pence and Trump are on the same page in opposing the runaway federal judiciary.

July 19, 2016

Why Evangelicals Should Support Trump

Many rank-and-file churchgoers overwhelmingly support Trump's views against current levels of immigration and trade. Evangelical voters preferred Trump over his rivals in the Republican primaries and they will surely vote heavily in favor of Trump rather than Hillary in the fall election. However, some church leaders still persist in supporting permissive immigration and opposing Trump. They are more likely to agree with Obama on immigration than with Donald Trump and their own congregations.

Two years ago, officials from several Christian denominations met with President Obama in the Oval Office and gushed their support of his so-called "immigration reform." Obama's phony "reform" means legislation that would grant citizenship to illegal aliens and do nothing to stem the flood of illegal immigrants coming to the U.S. Sadly, the immigration issue is preventing some church leaders from siding with Donald Trump. Prior Republican nominee Mitt Romney stridently criticized Donald Trump earlier this year. In fact, Romney still refuses to endorse him. This should not be a surprise because Romney had harshly criticized Trump's statements about immigration during the campaign.

Churchgoing voters showed their true feelings on this issue by nominating Donald Trump in the Republican primaries. Now is the time for church leaders to listen to their own flock on the important political issue of immigration. The immigration issue has become an elephant in the room that will be impossible to overlook in November. Church leaders should recognize that loving our neighbor does not mean unlocking our doors to any and all comers. When an unwelcome "neighbor" comes into our home, we "deport" him out of our house. The same principle should be used for our national borders. Trump's leadership on the immigration issue has earned him the support of millions of Democrats and Republicans.

Voters realize that Trump's immigration policy is the best way to protect Americans.

July 26, 2016
Trump's Speech Trumped Cruz

D onald Trump's acceptance speech proved that his vision, not Ted Cruz's, is the future of the conservative movement and the Republican Party. Trump hit the right notes in his talk in putting America first, while Cruz's presentation to the convention the night before was thin on conservative substance.

Cruz did not disqualify himself from being a future standard-bearer merely by failing to endorse Trump, but also by failing to embrace the conservative policies that are necessary to make America great again. It was Trump, not Cruz, who succeeded in fulfilling Ronald Reagan's goal of "raising a banner of no pale pastels, but bold colors which make it unmistakably clear where we stand on all of the issues troubling the people."

Trump repeatedly and passionately demonstrated in his acceptance speech that he would stand up for Americans and do everything in his power to end the exploitation of the United States by the rest of the world. "Americanism, not globalism, will be our credo!" Trump declared, adding that, "the American people will come first once again."

As Trump did throughout the campaign, he led on the fundamental issues of immigration and trade. While his rivals eventually followed his lead, it was Trump who framed the issues and forced the media to pay attention to them.

Trump explained in a compelling way the harm resulting from crime by illegal aliens. He described how he personally met with the family members of a young woman with a promising future who had been killed by an illegal alien who was then released and still remains at large in our country.

On jobs, the Republican Party since the 1990s supported free trade deals which have cost American workers dearly. Trump has single-handedly converted our party into one that is now pro-American-worker.

"I have visited the laid-off factory workers and the communities crushed by our horrible and unfair trade deals," Trump declared during his speech. "These are the forgotten men and women of our country ... who work hard but no longer have a voice."

"I am your voice," Trump then said, amid thunderous applause. For the first time since Ronald Reagan, the Republican Party has a nominee who actually represents the average American worker.

An astounding 12 million non-Republicans crossed party lines to vote for Trump in the Republican primaries. The Democrats did not vote for Trump because they prefer supporting a billionaire, but because they like his positions on immigration and trade.

Trump extolled "the dignity of work and the dignity of working people." He brings back to the Republican Party the "bricklayers, carpenters, and electricians" whom he said his father was most comfortable being with.

Trump observed that "America has lost nearly one-third of its manufacturing jobs since 1997," and that NAFTA was "one of the worst economic deals ever made by our country." "Never again," Trump added.

In contrast, Ted Cruz's speech at the convention made only passing references to immigration and trade, without the substance or the passion that Trump expressed. Instead Cruz repeated "freedom" over and over, some 23 times, declaring that "America is an ideal," and that the ideal is merely that "freedom matters."

Cruz's speech reflected the views of his mega-donors, who tend to be more libertarian than the conservative views of the average American. Leaving people alone to do whatever they like is not enough to restore the United States to military superiority or economic independence, or to achieve the many other goals set forth in the Republican Party Platform.

Cruz's vision is not that of Ronald Reagan, who made the United States stronger and more prosperous as Trump vows to do. Trump emphasized in his speech his opposition to the Trans-Pacific Partnership, which he said, "will not only destroy

PHYLLIS SCHLAFLY SPEAKS, VOLUME 2

our manufacturing, but it will make America subject to the rulings of foreign governments."

Trump even pledged "to never sign any trade agreement that hurts our workers, or that diminishes our freedom and independence." Cruz made no such pledge and failed to mention the Trans-Pacific Partnership.

Trump obviously meant every word in his electrifying speech, as when he expressed his genuine outrage at how "big business, elite media and major donors are lining up behind the campaign of [Hillary Clinton] because they know she will keep our rigged system in place." Cruz's speech had no such criticism of Hillary, and relied on superficial rhetorical devices like devoting much of his speech to a story about a sympathetic victim with whom Cruz had no personal connection.

The shortcoming of Ted Cruz is not only his failure to endorse the Republican Party nominee. The greater flaw is that, like Mitt Romney and others in the Republican Establishment, Cruz has failed to embrace the conservative vision that Donald Trump stands for.

August 2, 2016

Platforms Offer a Stark Choice

T he Republican and Democratic parties adopted new platforms at their conventions last month, and they have fundamentally different plans for America's future. The two major party platforms have not been this different from each other in our lifetimes.

A platform should be a statement of principles that can last for many years, not a partisan political attack against a particular candidate. The Republican Party platform has only one reference to Hillary Clinton and barely mentions Republican candidates of the past or present, while the Democratic Party Platform rants against Donald Trump 32 times.

The Democratic Party Platform wants federal taxpayer dollars to pay for abortions and for the first time calls for repealing the 40-year-old Hyde Amendment which limits federal spending on abortion. The Republican Party platform opposes the use of taxpayer dollars to fund abortion and declares that "the unborn child has a fundamental right to life."

The vacancy of conservative Justice Antonin Scalia hangs in the balance in this election, and the Democratic Party Platform tells us what their top priority is. When selecting the next Supreme Court justices and all future nominations to the federal bench, Democrats promise to appoint judges who will "protect" the abortion industry.

The Republican Platform explains that there is "a national crisis in our judiciary" due to activism by Democrat-appointed federal judges. "Only a Republican president will appoint judges who respect the rule of law expressed within the Constitution and Declaration of Independence, including the inalienable right to life and the laws of nature and nature's God, as did the late Justice Antonin Scalia," the GOP Platform explains.

The Republican Platform calls for "rebuilding the U.S. military into the strongest on earth, with vast superiority over any other nation or group of nations in the world." The

Democrats' platform does not mention military superiority or "American exceptionalism," but blames Americans for a "recent uptick in Islamophobia."

A quarter of the Republican Party Platform is devoted to a section entitled "America Resurgent," which sets forth the steps necessary to restore peace through strength while heeding "the wisdom of President George Washington's warning to avoid foreign entanglements and unnecessary alliances." The Democratic Platform calls for enmeshing the United States in a "global network of alliances."

Republicans support women's "exemption from direct ground combat units and infantry battalions" and "reject the use of the military as a platform for social experimentation." Democrats say, "We are proud of the opening of combat positions to women. Our military is strongest when people of all sexual orientations and gender identities are honored for their service to our country."

The Democratic Platform opposes "voter identification laws," which Democrats falsely describe as discriminatory. Americans are routinely required to show photo ID to board airplanes and enter government buildings, and the integrity of our elections is important enough to require meaningful verification of identity and citizenship before casting a ballot.

The Republican Platform, for the first time, calls for building a wall to stop the overrunning of our southern border by illegal aliens: "We support building a wall along our southern border and protecting all ports of entry." The platform explains that amid "terrorism, drug cartels, human trafficking, and criminal gangs, the presence of millions of unidentified individuals in this country poses grave risks to the safety and sovereignty of the United States."

In contrast, the Democrats demand amnesty for the many millions of foreigners who entered our country illegally or failed to go home on time, a policy that simply encourages millions more to do likewise. The Democratic Platform would grant driver's licenses, in-state tuition, and citizenship for millions of illegals in our country, the vast majority of whom would then be loyal voters for the Democratic Party.

The Republican Platform says, "We need better negotiated trade agreements that put America first. When trade agreements do not adequately protect U.S. sovereignty, they must be rejected," declining to endorse the Trans-Pacific Partnership, which the Democratic Platform allows.

"These are the standards Democrats believe must be applied to all trade agreements, including the Trans-Pacific Partnership," is a face-saving sentence in the Democrats' platform that gives Hillary Clinton the green light to approve it with minor modifications. Last week one of her top allies, Terry McAuliffe, confirmed that a President Hillary Clinton would embrace this horrible deal, and then he tried to deny it amid an intense backlash.

Teachers' unions are the backbone of the Democratic Party, and its platform omits any reference to homeschooling. The Republican Platform extols the benefits of parental control over education, and praises multiple alternatives to the failing public school system.

The sharp contrast between the Republican and Democratic platforms leaves no room for doubt about which party should receive your vote in November.

August 16, 2016
Lesson of "The Snake"

L ast week in Erie, Pennsylvania, Donald Trump entertained his vast crowd of supporters by reciting the lyrics to a song called "The Snake." The song was written about 50 years ago, but it tells a timeless truth derived from Aesop's Fables, which are more than 2,500 years old.

The song tells the story of a "tender-hearted woman" who rescues a "poor, half-frozen snake" from near-death in the winter cold. "Take me in, oh tender woman," the snake cries out. "Take me in, for heaven's sake."

So the tender-hearted woman takes the snake into her own home, warms it by the fire and feeds it milk and honey: "If I hadn't brought you in, by now you might have died." But instead of saying thanks, the snake gave her a vicious bite.

"I saved you," cried the woman. "And you've bitten me, but why? You know your bite is poisonous, and now I'm going to die." "Oh shut up, silly woman," said the reptile with a grin. "You knew damn well I was a snake before you took me in."

The moral of the song was clear to many in the crowd, but Donald Trump made sure that everyone got the message. "This is what is going on in our country, with our border," he told the 9,000 people who filled the Erie Insurance Arena.

"When you're listening to this, think of our border. Think of the people we are letting in by the thousands. And Hillary Clinton wants to allow 550 percent more coming in to our country. How stupid are we!"

That's right: Hillary wants to bring in 65,000 Syrian refugees, which is indeed a 550 percent increase over the 10,000 who entered this year, which in turn is a 500 percent increase over last year's intake of about 1,600. Obama is now rushing to complete his pledge to bring in 10,000 Syrian refugees by September 30, despite FBI Director Comey's testimony last October that those people can't be vetted because there are no reliable records on them.

As Trump said at the rally in Erie, "We want to help people, but we can't take a chance. We know bad things are going to happen. We know, as we allow more and more people to come in from terror areas, bad things are going to happen."

To illustrate the "bad things" that are bound to happen when "we allow more and more people to come in from terror areas," Senator Jeff Sessions (R-AL) last week released the names of 20 people convicted of terrorism in the last three years after being admitted to our country as refugees from such countries as Iraq, Somalia, Uzbekistan and Bosnia. One of the 20 had received a special visa for Iraqi translators and subsequently became a U.S. citizen, yet he pledged an oath to the leader of ISIS.

Trump's compassionate solution for the refugee crisis is to "build a beautiful safe zone in Syria" and get the so-called Gulf States to pay for it. The Gulf States are the oil-rich kingdoms of the Persian Gulf whose existence is protected by the U.S. Navy, but have contributed nothing for the welfare of their fellow Arab Muslims in need.

"The story of 'The Snake' is what's happening to our country," Trump continued. "We're letting people in. Many of these people hate us. Many of these people don't have good thoughts. And you see what one sick wacko can do in Orlando. And then you see his father sitting behind Hillary Clinton with a big smile on his face."

That's right, the father of Omar Mateen, who murdered 49 people at the Pulse nightclub on June 12, was allowed to sit directly behind Hillary where he was visible on camera during her entire 25-minute speech. Seddique Matteen, who apparently came to the United States as a refugee in the 1980s, told reporters that Hillary Clinton "would be good for the United States, versus Donald Trump."

Before we allow any more refugees from Syria, let's take a closer look at what happened to a previous wave of refugees brought here from the East African failed state of Somalia. Starting in the 1990s, an estimated 100,000 Muslims from Somalia have been resettled in Minnesota and Maine at U.S. taxpayers' expense.

Instead of expressing their gratitude for the opportunity to live in a peaceful, prosperous nation, many Somalis have been trained by leftist community organizers to adopt an entitlement mentality, quick to complain about alleged discrimination. If that's not bad enough, a disproportionate number of their young men have supported terrorism or have even traveled overseas to join ISIS.

※

August 23, 2016
Why We Need a Tough President

I t is becoming clearer than ever that the United States needs a president who will be tough on the issue of immigration. It is always American citizens who pay the price when the Administration does not take immigration seriously. That was the case for Casey Chadwick. She was stabbed to death in her apartment last year by an illegal Haitian immigrant named Jean Jacques. A report released by the Inspector General showed what led to her tragic death. Immigration and Customs Enforcement should have deported Jacques long before the murder of Chadwick ever occurred. Jacques entered the U.S. illegally in 1992. He served 15 years in prison for attempted murder. He was later jailed again for violating his parole. Clearly, Jacques did not belong on American soil.

ICE is not the only agency at fault in this failure. The DHS reported that ICE tried to deport Jacques 3 times. Each time Haiti refused to take back their own citizen. Haiti did not want to deal with their criminals, so they sent the criminals to us. That is why America needs a president who will make immigration a priority. The president and his State Department has the ability to threaten sanctions against nations who will not take back their own criminals. These threats have been successful in the past.

This report from the Inspector General should serve as a warning on America's most pressing campaign issue. Immigration is not just an issue of policy. Immigration is an issue of public safety. Americans should be able to sleep at night without fear of attack by violent criminal illegal aliens.

Trump is the only presidential candidate who understands the immigration issue and how to solve it. Trump has the boldness and willpower to make countries take back their criminals. That is the kind of boldness and willpower that we need in the oval office to handle immigration policy.

⤬

August 29, 2016
Learning From Tragedy

The Orlando shooting which resulted in the deaths of 49 innocent people was the largest mass shooting in American history. This tragic loss of life has many Americans wondering what must be done to stop the trend of violence. People have to understand what motivated Omar Mateen to carry out this attack. Unfortunately, the Left is only concerned with maintaining their political agenda. They are willing to do anything to keep people from acknowledging that Omar Mateen was acting on behalf of radical Islam.

Planned Parenthood said, "Islam doesn't foment the violence alleged gunman Omar Mateen enacted, toxic masculinity and a global culture of imperialist homophobia does." This statement shows how willfully ignorant the liberals are. Mateen's violent hatred of women, homosexuals, and minorities is a characteristic of radical Islam. We cannot address the terrorism issue without identifying what causes it.

The Orlando shooting was an act of radical Islamic terrorism. Mateen said so himself by pledging allegiance to ISIS while carrying out the attack. However, President Obama and the Left refuse to acknowledge the role of radical Islam. They would rather blame the attack on guns and gun activists. Their solution is to ban guns like the AR-15, which was not even used in the attack.

Acknowledging the role of radical Islam is the first step to dealing with mass terrorist shootings. The United States needs to stop bringing in so many Muslim immigrants like Mateen's parents until we know how to handle them. Donald Trump's proposed ban on Muslim immigrants is the best solution for the danger that we face. A Hillary Clinton presidency will leave America vulnerable to more deadly attacks from Islamic radicals.

We need a Commander-In-Chief who will call out the enemy by name and confront them with the full force of America's strength. We need a president who will take seriously the issue of radical Islamic terrorism.

September 6, 2016
Trump in Mexico Recalls Reagan in Geneva

D onald Trump's surprise visit to Mexico, where he met the Mexican president and discussed the many contentious issues between our two countries, reminds me of President Reagan's important trip to Geneva in 1985. Reagan was more than willing to sit down with the Communist leader in an effort to build a personal connection between the two men without sacrificing America's vital interests in the Cold War.

The 1985 Geneva summit was highly advertised as a potential showdown between Reagan and Gorbachev, the supposedly reasonable new Soviet leader. When it was over, Americans realized that behind Reagan's genial affability was a steely determination to protect our country against the threat of Soviet nuclear missiles.

Just as today's mainstream media is bent on undermining Trump's call to put Americans first in our dealings with Mexico, the media of the 1980s (led by ABC's Sam Donaldson and CBS's Dan Rather) were overwhelmingly pro-Gorbachev and anti-Reagan in their daily coverage.

Left-wing celebrities from around the world converged on Geneva to support the media narrative that a stubborn President Reagan was refusing to consider Gorbachev's reasonable proposals for world peace. Congresswoman Bella Abzug, actress Jane Alexander and the inevitable Jesse Jackson were giving daily interviews.

I led a delegation of 25 distinguished women leaders to Geneva to support Reagan and American nuclear superiority. The media didn't give us much coverage, but President Reagan telephoned me afterwards from the White House to thank me for our support.

Reagan had been elected on a promise to "win" the Cold War against the Communist forces arrayed against America. Before Reagan, our country's foreign policy was controlled by men like Henry Kissinger, who thought victory was impossible and that his job, as he famously told Admiral Zumwalt, was "to negotiate the most acceptable second-best position" for the United States.

After three decades of steady deterioration of America's place in the world, Trump is the first candidate since Reagan who is comfortable using Reagan's vocabulary of winning. Trump has pledged to make America "win" again, instead of being cheated and outmaneuvered by our adversaries and even our so-called allies.

Trump's visit to Mexico recalls Reagan's trip to Geneva in other ways too. At both meetings, there was one signature position on which the American refused to budge.

Reagan's no-surrender pledge was his unwavering commitment to the Strategic Defense Initiative, that is, to build and deploy a system to shoot down Soviet nuclear missiles headed for our cities. With Trump, it's his rock-solid promise to build "an impenetrable physical wall" on our southern border.

Both Reagan's and Trump's signature ideas were purely defensive weapons to which no country could have any legitimate complaint. Reagan's SDI was a non-nuclear weapon whose only function was to destroy or deflect incoming nuclear missiles.

Reagan stuck to that non-negotiable position at the summit with Gorbachev the following year in Reykjavik, Iceland. As we now know, that's when Gorby realized he could never win an open competition with the United States, so that his "acceptable second-best position" was the dissolution of the USSR over the next five years.

Likewise, Donald Trump's wall is not a provocative, but a neighborly idea to stop the rampant illegality that harms both nations along the U.S.-Mexico border. With no legitimate objection to erecting a fence, wall or other physical barrier between our two countries, Mexico should be grateful for Trump's leadership and even agree to help pay for it.

The value of a wall begins with stopping "murderers" and "rapists" from freely entering and re-entering our country with impunity, as Trump mentioned when he announced the start of his campaign last year, but it doesn't stop there. Felony assault by motor vehicle is another deadly crime that seems to be rampant by illegal aliens driving recklessly without the licenses or insurance that law-abiding Americans take for granted.

The wall would also stop the plague of heroin that has exploded during the last few years of the Obama administration. Deaths from heroin overdoses surpassed deaths from car crashes last year and will hit a new record this year. Most U.S. heroin is delivered by Mexicans working for the drug cartels.

Of course, most Mexican immigrants are not murderers, rapists, drunk drivers or drug dealers. But even the good, hard-working people who come here from south of the border, both legally and illegally, have such low education and skills that they can't survive economically without massive public subsidies to provide for the care, food, shelter, health care, education and welfare of their children.

Voters finally have the opportunity to choose a president who will make America first by securing our border and ending one-sided trade deals that favor foreign workers rather than our own.

Trump's strong stance in his meeting with the Mexican president demonstrates that Donald Trump is the "choice, not an echo."

About Phyllis Schlafly

Phyllis Schlafly was a national leader of the conservative movement since the publication of her best-selling 1964 book, *A Choice Not An Echo* which was updated and re-issued in 2014. She was a leader of the pro-family movement since 1972, when she started her national volunteer organization called Eagle Forum. The *Ladies' Home Journal* named her one of the 100 most important women of the 20th century.

Mrs. Schlafly is the author or editor of 27 books and served as a member of the Commission on the Bicentennial of the U.S. Constitution, 1985-1991, appointed by President Reagan. She has testified before more than 50 Congressional and State Legislative committees on constitutional, national defense, and family issues.

Phyllis Schlafly is America's best-known advocate of the dignity and honor that we as a society owe to the role of full-time homemaker. The mother of six children, she was the 1992 Illinois Mother of the Year. She passed away on September 5, 2016.

About Ed Martin

On September 28, 2015, Phyllis Schlafly named Ed Martin as her hand-picked successor. Ed had been working as a special assistant to Phyllis for more than two years. A lawyer and bioethicist by training, Ed had previously served as chairman of the Missouri Republican Party and chief of staff to Missouri Governor Matt Blunt. Ed lives in St. Louis, Missouri, with his wife and four children.